TAME YOUR ANXIETY

TAME YOUR ANXIETY

Rewiring Your Brain for Happiness

LORETTA GRAZIANO BREUNING

ROWMAN & LITTLEFIELD
Lanham • Boulder • New York • London

Published by Rowman & Littlefield
An imprint of The Rowman & Littlefield Publishing Group, Inc.
4501 Forbes Boulevard, Suite 200, Lanham, Maryland 20706
www.rowman.com

6 Tinworth Street, London SE11 5AL, United Kingdom

Distributed by NATIONAL BOOK NETWORK

British Library Cataloguing in Publication Information Available

Library of Congress Cataloging-in-Publication Data

Names: Breuning, Loretta Graziano, author.
Title: Tame your anxiety : rewiring your brain for happiness / Loretta
    Graziano Breuning.
Description: Lanham : Rowman & Littlefield, [2019] | Includes bibliographical
    references and index.
Identifiers: LCCN 2018047271 (print) | LCCN 2018047913 (ebook) | ISBN
    9781538117774 (electronic) | ISBN 9781538117767 (pbk. : alk. paper)
Subjects: LCSH: Happiness—Physiological aspects. |
    Neurotransmitters—Popular works. | Self-care, Health—Popular works.
Classification: LCC QP401 (ebook) | LCC QP401 .B75 2019 (print) | DDC
    612.8/23342—dc23
LC record available at https://lccn.loc.gov/2018047271

♾™ The paper used in this publication meets the minimum requirements of American National Standard for Information Sciences—Permanence of Paper for Printed Library Materials, ANSI/NISO Z39.48-1992.

Printed in the United States of America

For my grandchild,
Josephine Lorraine Breuning Evans

CONTENTS

Introduction   1

1   What Is Tame?   7

2   What Is Anxiety?   13

3   A Taming Tool That Works   25

4   Your Power over Your Brain   43

5   Design the Tool That's Right for You   57

6   Keeping It Tame in the Long Run   75

7   Stock Your Pantry with Anxiety Tamers   87

8   Avoid These Six Pitfalls   105

9   Food and Anxiety   119

10 Help Others Tame Anxiety   131

Epilogue   141

Bibliography   143

Index   145

Keep in Touch   147

Introduction

MY CLOSE ENCOUNTER WITH CORTISOL

I changed a powerless feeling to a powerful feeling by focusing on the power I had.

Anxiety can start from something small and spiral into something big. This happened to me recently, and it helped me build new skills.

The spiral started when I tried to clean up a messy pile on my desk. I had ignored the pile for months because I was busy with a project. Now the project was finished and the pile started to bother me. I decided to invest time cleaning it up. I picked up the paper on the top of the pile, but it required a decision I wasn't ready to make. So I pulled a sheet from the middle of the stack. That one stymied me too. After a few minutes of frustration, the pile didn't get any smaller and I decided to do it "tomorrow." The next day, just looking at the pile gave me a bad feeling. Those old papers held reminders of old frustrations, disappointments, and failures.

The same thing happened with my sock drawer. It jammed when I tried to close it because it was too full. I ignored this when I was busy with the project, but now that I had time, I stopped to fix it. I picked up a sock that I rarely used and thought about where to put it. I wondered why my life no longer required this sock, and whether that would change. I couldn't answer that question, so I moved on to another sock. A bad feeling turned on that was curiously familiar. I grew up seeing my mother rage when she tried to shut an overstuffed drawer. I felt powerless and scared when my mother raged. Now my socks were triggering that feeling despite my good intentions.

Decluttering became a fad around this time. Everyone seemed to be reading a book about "tidying up." I didn't aspire to be "tidy," but there were junk zones in my house that upset me whenever I passed them. Everyone else seemed to be enjoying the decluttered life, and I wanted it too. I set the intention and read the book.

But each time I tried to winnow my clutter, bad feelings surged. I am usually decisive, but when I entered my junk zones, I couldn't even decide where to put a paper clip. Would I need paper clips in the future? I didn't think so, but I wasn't ready to give up the possibility of such a future either. Each item raised uncomfortable questions about my future. The bad feeling got worse when I saw dust bunnies beneath the clutter. They gave me a sense of urgency that I kept failing to relieve.

I seized on the idea of giving stuff to my kids so I could happily imagine my stuff having a future. But my kids rejected the offer with an absolute "no!"

I was stuck. I accepted that I had a problem and needed help.

So I turned to the wisdom of the internet. I searched on the words "decluttering services," and stumbled on a blog post called "Why Your Kids Don't Want Your Stuff." The author of the post seemed to understand me. She was a local home-organizing consultant, so I called for an appointment. I told her I just wanted a one-hour chat rather than the full OCD treatment. Her minimum was two hours, so I went with that.

Those two hours changed everything. She asked me what I love to do but never make time for. I said I wanted to read the books that were piled up everywhere. She told me to spend a half hour decluttering and then a half hour reading. She pushed me to schedule these decluttering sessions on my calendar. I chose to do three a week. As I typed it in my calendar, I was excited about the books I would read.

The consultant wanted me to continue until the whole house was done, but I only wanted to clear up my junk zones. She strongly advised against that, and I strongly refused her advice. Suddenly, I had a sense of clarity about my future. I liked having a project. I did not want to be a neatnik. I couldn't wait to relieve the clutter so I could start on my next project. I had been stalled because I was waiting for support. I realized that I needed to start a new project with or without support. I would start as soon as I cleared up those junk zones, with or without the consultant's approval. Suddenly, I was eager to clean them up.

I defined the goal precisely: to clear up my desk, sock drawer, and five other disaster areas around the house. Clearing up means emptying them entirely so they could be cleaned, and then refilling them 90 percent so I'd always have some free space. I imagined the serenity I'd enjoy when it was done.

I disagreed with the consultant on another issue: recycling. She wanted me to throw things in the garbage and I couldn't stand to do that. I hired her with the assumption that she'd know good places to donate items. But the more I raised the issue, the more she insisted that I would never get it done unless I put things in the garbage. The more she said that, the more I realized that I needed to find a good home for my stuff in order to feel good about decluttering. It might slow me down, but I would finish, and I would enjoy knowing my junk had a future.

I invited my husband to the sit-down with the consultant. I had mixed motives, I confess. I could say I was being considerate, since it was his home too. But I was also hoping for help. My husband was kind enough to join the conversation, but he did not pull out his calendar. He was busy with his own projects and the mess in my closets was not his problem. As much as I longed to be rescued from this burden, I realized that I could do it faster without him. It was my junk, and my anxiety about the junk.

Two months later, I finished! I felt pride instead of fear and shame whenever I looked at those junk zones. I loved having a clean place to put things. I loved my new tool for tackling junk the next time it accumulates. Best of all, I could use that tool any time a little irritant spiraled into big anxiety.

WHAT WORKED?

The bad feeling I had when I looked at my clutter was caused by *cortisol*. This chemical is the brain's signal that your survival is threatened. Of course I didn't consciously believe my survival was threatened, but cortisol makes it feel that way. Surprisingly big cortisol surges can spiral from surprisingly small triggers. Threatened feelings are easier to manage when you know how this happens. Let's take a closer look.

The first trigger was free time. When you are busy putting out fires, small cortisol trickles are easy to ignore. But when nothing big is going on, these drips get your attention.

The second trigger was old pain. I was constantly exposed to my mother's pain growing up. Early cortisol experiences build the neural pathways that turn on bad feelings later on.

Social comparison was the third trigger. I imagined everyone else tidying up successfully. I wanted the decluttered life I believed everyone else had.

Existential fear was the next trigger. We are all aware of our own mortality and we usually manage the fear by avoiding it. But it tends to creep in when you think about the future and squarely face decisions about how to allocate the time you have left.

Taking responsibility was the last trigger. I longed to shift the burden to my kids or my husband or even a stranger. That might not solve the long-run problem, but it can relieve the cortisol of the moment. When my burden-shifting strategies failed, I had to face my own reality.

Cortisol is an ancient chemical found in mammals, reptiles, fish, mollusks, amoeba, and even plants! It evolved to do a job: to alert you to potential threats so you can act in time to protect yourself. It tells your brain to scan for potential threat signals, and prepares your body for action. Cortisol does its job by making you feel bad, so you do what it takes to make it stop. But you don't always know how. So there you are flooded with threat signals ready to act without a plan that works. That can lead to more cortisol, more evidence of threat, and more cortisol. Soon you're in a bad loop.

I knew the junk on my desk was not a big threat, but each failure to manage it boosted my cortisol. This fit the pattern of my early cortisol circuits, which led to more cortisol. That triggered social fears and mortality fears, and more cortisol. The chemical created a sense of crisis in my body even though my verbal brain didn't think it was a crisis.

I turned the ship around by imagining a solution and stepping toward it. Each step was small, but I felt good as soon as I saw myself approaching a goal. Old frustrations were still there, but they didn't feel like crises when I had a sense of where I was going. Decluttering was suddenly a step toward a goal instead of a threat.

At first, the new steps were hard to take, so rewarding myself with downtime was very motivating. I looked forward to my half hour of reading tremendously. I knew my decluttering session would end with a relaxed feeling. But that wasn't enough sometimes. After a hard day of work, I didn't always feel calm enough to sort through old albatrosses. On those days, I did a half hour of reading *before* the decluttering. Sometimes I did it before *and* after! You may think it's cheating, but life is not a race against the clock. It's a quest to feel good in the short run while doing things that are healthy in the long run. Eventually, my brain learned to associate decluttering with a good feeling rather than a bad feeling.

On a deeper level, I changed a powerless feeling to a powerful feeling. My power is limited, of course. I don't have the power to transcend mortality, or push my junk onto others, or change my past, or force people to support my projects. Instead of dwelling on powerless feelings, I focused on the power I have. I can clear the decks for my next project and get excited about it. I can take a new view of past failures that my junk reminds me of. I can celebrate my freedom to make my own decisions.

We all long for free time, but cortisol often seeps into free time. Small irritants cascade as your brain zooms in on potential threats. It's hard to find the exit when you're in this loop. This is why people resist taking the free time they need.

There is a better way. You can train your brain to shift from a cortisol loop to a happy loop. This book describes a simple tool for doing that, which rests on the same basic elements as my decluttering strategy. You will learn to

1. focus on meeting your needs
2. break challenges into small chunks
3. reward yourself for your steps

Anxiety is a cortisol spiral. Once you're in it, it's hard to take the steps you need to get out of it. But if you practice this taming tool every day, it will come to you automatically in moments of distress. You will define your needs and step toward them, and your good feelings will flow. Your brain will learn to expect a good feeling instead of a bad feeling. You will tame your anxiety.

1

WHAT IS TAME?

You can tame the relationship between your horse and rider.

The word *tame* has many negative associations. I think of a "lion tamer" with a whip and a chair. That is not how I want to treat my brain! "The Taming of the Shrew" is another unattractive image. Where can we find a positive image of "tame"?

A tame animal, like a pet, may seem appealing at first. But pets lack basic survival skills as a result of domestication. They do not use their brain for the job it evolved for—finding food, avoiding threats, and managing social alliances. They spend their adulthood in childlike dependence, often at the expense of their reproductive system. You do not want that kind of tame.

Philosophers often compare the mind to a rider struggling to tame a horse (or elephant or donkey). It's tempting to think of anxiety as a wild horse. But this analogy suggests an acrimonious relationship between horse and rider. The horse resists the rider's harsh control. The horse blames the rider and the rider blames the horse. You cannot tame your anxiety by pitting your horse and rider against each other.

But you can tame the relationship between your horse and rider. This is the positive approach to anxiety.

We humans have two brains. On the outside, we have a spaghetti of neurons that is unique to humans, but on the inside, we have the same core structures that all mammals have in common (the amygdala, hippocampus, thalamus, and so on, collectively called the limbic system). Your two brains must get along in order to have a good quality of life. Tame the relationship between your verbal brain and your mammalian operating system and you will enjoy the ride wherever you go.

Here is a simple example. Imagine a rider frantically flailing at a horse that refuses to budge. Now imagine a steep cliff on the trail ahead. The rider doesn't see it because it's not on the trail map. The horse sees it, so the pair will survive if the rider accepts the horse's knowledge. They're in trouble if the rider focuses only on the map and ignores the horse.

But sometimes the horse is wrong. Imagine a horse running wild after seeing a snake. Survival depends on the horse accepting guidance from the rider. But the rider must communicate in a way that the horse understands instead of just in words.

Communication between the verbal brain and the animal brain is a huge challenge. Let's say the rider offers a carrot to the agitated horse. Carrots are like candy to a horse. A big reward builds a big connection in the mammal brain, wiring it to seek more rewards in the ways that worked before. So, the next day, the horse acts frenzied in the spot where it got the carrot. The well-meaning rider offers another carrot. A day later, it takes two carrots to stop the frenzy. The animal brain is just doing the job it evolved for—repeating behaviors that get rewards.

Taming the relationship between your horse and rider is a challenge when your horse runs wild, but if you soothe it with sweet rewards it might make things worse. How can your big spaghetti of neurons guide your inner mammal through a world full of snakes?

You have to communicate with your inner mammal in a way that it understands. This book shows you how. You will learn about the brain chemicals that motivate it, and the neural pathways that control these chemicals. You will discover your power over these neural pathways so you can guide your inner mammal from unhappy to happy chemicals. To do this, you will have to blaze a trail that's not on your map.

Sometimes there's a cliff on your path and your horse's agitation can save you. Other times, the agitation is just a bad carrot habit. You must constantly interpret your horse's responses in order to choose your best next step. The more you know about the mammal brain, the better you can choose.

TAME IN NATURE

If you were a gazelle, your cortisol would be triggered by the smell of a lion. That would motivate you to run, and escape would relieve your cortisol. If you were a gazelle, hunger would trigger your cortisol, and finding food would relieve it. In nature, bad feelings are tamed by meeting needs and avoiding harm. But a gazelle is never completely safe from predator threat and hunger. Why doesn't it surge with cortisol all the time? Because natural selection built a brain that promotes survival. Constant anxiety would not promote a gazelle's survival. The brain built by natural selection is always analyzing the situation and deciding when cortisol would promote survival.

A gazelle doesn't do its analyzing with words and abstractions. It does it with neural pathways. The cortisol spurts of its youth built pathways that turn on its cortisol today. The happy-chemical spurts of its youth likewise built pathways that turn on happy chemicals in similar future circumstances. In each moment, a gazelle is weighing its options with the pathways it has.

For example, a gazelle does not always run when it sees a lion. It knows the difference between a lion on the prowl and a lion just passing through. A gazelle would rather keep eating than run from every potential threat signal. It needs to eat a lot of grass to survive. On the other hand, a little hunger is better than instant death. The gazelle brain is constantly taking in the evidence available to its senses. Those sensory inputs flow down the neural pathways it has. When inputs match past threats, electricity flows to the "on" switch of its cortisol, and the gazelle acts to relieve the cortisol. When the inputs do not match past threats, electricity keeps flowing to the reward of eating grass.

Your brain is constantly responding to the world with neural pathways built from your past experience. Your pathways are similar to a gazelle's in some ways and different in others. They are similar to those of other people in some ways but also unique. You have more power over your neural pathways when you understand them. You can blaze new trails in your brain to enjoy more good feelings and relieve more bad feelings.

We humans often want to change ourselves. A gazelle never feels the need to change. It just accepts its neurochemical responses without judging them. Gazelles are not happy all the time the way you might think. Sometimes a gazelle sees its child get eaten alive. Sometimes it drinks at a waterhole next to the predator that ate its child. But a gazelle does not dream of disconnecting its internal alarm system. It honors the valuable survival information. It strives to turn it off the way nature intended: by escaping threats and seeking rewards.

Life is different when you have a big spaghetti of extra neurons. Our big cortex allows us to anticipate future threats instead of just waiting until the threat is upon us. Predators don't eat our babies because we anticipate threats in time to prevent them. But we end up feeling threatened a lot.

If you tamed your anxiety the way a gazelle does, you would spend your day eating and reproducing, and ignore threats until they were about to get you. The flaw in this strategy is obvious to your big cortex. It is so skilled at anticipating threats that it even sees how today's pleasures can cause tomorrow's threats. We humans build neural pathways that anticipate future consequences instead of just focusing on immediate rewards and threats. These pathways shape our eating and reproductive behavior, leaving us with diets, grooming rituals, and PTA meetings that gazelles don't have. They shape our threat perceptions, motivating an endless quest for "news." But all that anticipating doesn't relieve our sense of threat. On the contrary. When we succeed at taking action to relieve a potential threat, our cortex skillfully moves on to the next potential threat.

BLAZING A NEW TRAIL

Anxiety is just a trail in your brain. It's a neural pathway connecting an input pattern to your cortisol's on switch. You have a lot of these pathways because you have a lot of experience with potential threats. But some of your pathways have grown huge because you've used them so often.

Taming anxiety means blazing a new trail in your brain—a trail that leads to your happy chemicals instead of your threat chemicals. That is hard to do for many reasons. You don't know how to build trails because your old ones weren't built intentionally. You don't feel safe when you leave the trails you know. And it seems like a lot of work.

But the trails you have lead to a bad place sometimes. You can imagine a better place. You can get there by learning to build a new trail.

Yes, it's work. But this book shows you how to make that work effective. You will learn to design the trail that's right for you, to stimulate your happy chemicals in moments when you feel threatened. Your trailblazing effort will be richly rewarded.

There is no one perfect trail. This book has no secret trail map to offer. It helps you discover your unique trails, and reroute them toward your unique happy circuits.

YOUR POWER OVER YOUR BRAIN

You may find it hard to believe that your feelings come from trails in your brain. Our feelings seem urgent and real, so it's hard to think of them as accidental connections between neurons. Of course your feelings are real in the sense that a real chemical molecule is released that triggers a real physical response in your body. We presume these responses are real information about the world around us because that's how the mammal brain is designed to work.

Your verbal cortex struggles to make sense of your mammalian responses. The cortex has no insider information about the mammal brain it's attached to, as unbelievable as that seems. Your verbal mind just guesses at the reason for a neurochemical spurt based on past experience. Sometimes it just ignores the spurts.

But your neurochemicals are powerful. They evolved to create urgent impulses to approach rewards and escape harm. They make you feel like it's a matter of life and death because brains that did that survived and their children survived. This is why life-and-death feelings creep up on us without our conscious awareness. You almost feel like they didn't come from you because your verbal inner voice did not decide to turn them on. When you understand the relationship between your two brains, you can improve that relationship.

Each of us is born with billions of neurons but very few connections between them. The connections we build shape the responses we have. Fortunately, you can build new connections by feeding your brain new experiences. But it's a conundrum: how can you have new experiences with the old pathways?

This conundrum explains why you can't just relax when someone tells you to "just relax!" Your brain is not designed to just relax. It's designed to seek rewards and avoid harm. A gazelle does not survive by relaxing.

Nothing is wrong with you. You are using your brain for the job it evolved for: to promote your survival by responding to the world with a sense of urgency.

And yet, we long for relief from the endless anticipation of threats and lost rewards. I learned about this longing as a docent at my local zoo. Visitors often asked me whether animals break out of the zoo, and I had to tell them that more animals break in than break out. What animal wouldn't want to get into a place where all your needs are met effortlessly?

But our brain did not evolve for life in a zoo. It does not release happy chemicals when your needs are met by a zookeeper. The more you know about your happy chemicals, the better you can blaze a trail that turns them on in healthy ways.

A gazelle's happy chemicals turn on when it steps toward meeting its needs. It feels good before the grass is digested and the nutrition is absorbed. Just seeing a patch of green grass turns on the good feeling, and that initiates a step toward it. A gazelle does not need a world of perfect safety to feel good. It only needs to step toward rewards with no immediate threat.

The mammal brain rewards you with a good feeling when you take a step. It is not designed to reward you for imagining yourself on a tropical beach. It rewards you for actual steps toward rewards or away from harm.

We can't guarantee that our steps are the right ones, of course. Our big brain anticipates possible missteps. A gazelle expects its steps to succeed because they have succeeded before. It has escaped a predator before. It has found grass before. It anticipates relief, and if it doesn't come, cortisol keeps surging and new steps are tried. Gazelles die young, but they don't imagine everything going wrong while they're alive. They don't have enough neurons to do that.

We do. We have enough neurons to imagine missteps that we have never actually experienced. Our imagined threats feel real enough to trigger our cortisol. But we can also imagine new steps that tame our cortisol.

REMEMBER:

1. We have two brains—a spaghetti of neurons that is unique to humans (the cortex), and a standard mammalian operating system (the amygdala, hippocampus, thalamus, etc.).
2. Your mammal brain controls the chemicals that make you feel good or bad. If you want to feel good, you have to get it from your mammal brain.
3. Natural selection built a brain that is focused on survival. It rewards you with a good-feeling chemical when you meet a survival need and a bad-feeling chemical when you see a survival threat.
4. We define rewards and threats with neural pathways built from experience. Your pathways build each time your reward chemicals and threat chemicals are released.
5. The human cortex can construct abstractions instead of being limited to the information that comes in from your eyes or ears or hands. The future is an abstraction and the cortex constructs information about the future.
6. The brain anticipates threats in order to prevent them and thus feel safe.
7. We anticipate threats with neural pathways built from past threats.
8. The brain anticipates rewards and motivates steps toward them. A reward is anything you expect to meet a need.
9. Our brain evolved to promote survival so it creates life-and-death feelings about meeting your needs and avoiding potential threats.

2

WHAT IS ANXIETY?

You don't consciously think your sock drawer can kill you, but cortisol creates the feeling that you will die if you don't make it stop.

A nxiety is cortisol triggered by the perception of threat.

Our threat perceptions can be mystifying until you know some biology. The fight-or-flight response was discovered in the early twentieth century by Walter B. Cannon. Of course, people had always seen animals fight and flee. What Cannon discovered was the way brain chemicals cause these behaviors.

Cannon and his colleagues at Harvard Medical School were studying animal responses to better understand disease in humans. They usually studied one thing at a time, but when they explored the body's response to cortisol and catecholamines (adrenaline), they uncovered a startling array of diverse responses: the heart speeds, digestion slows, the breath accelerates, and simultaneous changes occur in the eyes, ears, skin, liver, reproductive system, and immune system. In his autobiography, Cannon describes his bewilderment at these discoveries. Why would the body produce many seemingly unrelated physical responses at the same time?

Cannon realized that each of these changes prepare an animal to manage a threat. He called it the "fight-or-flight response" in his 1915 book, *Bodily Changes in Pain, Hunger, Fear, and Rage.* This insight may seem obvious today, since we know how the story ends, but it was a huge insight at the time. In fact it was three insights:

- that the separate physical responses are a coordinated preparation for managing threat;
- that the different responses are triggered by the same chemicals; and
- that these physiological responses in animals are the stuff of emotion in humans.

This chapter zooms in on the cortisol response to illuminate our anxious emotions. You can help your horse and rider communicate when you understand the job that cortisol is designed to do. We will not focus on adrenaline, so the difference between adrenaline and cortisol must be explained. Let's say you hear a noise and you wonder if it signals danger. You freeze to listen closer and interpret information. Adrenaline creates the awareness that something relevant to your survival may be happening and you should focus completely on it. Cortisol is only released if you decide that the noise is actually a threat.

Public speaking is another familiar example. Before you start speaking, adrenaline revs you up with excitement. After you speak, cortisol is released if you think it went badly. Adrenaline evolved to prepare your body for immediate action, while cortisol's job is to pump you up for a sustained struggle. We will focus on cortisol here because it's the chemical most directly associated with the perception of threat.

Cortisol is not a philosophical thought. It's the full-body sensation that you are facing a mortal threat. You don't consciously think your sock drawer can kill you, of course, but cortisol creates the feeling that you will die if you don't make it stop.

Cortisol turns on when you see cues that fit the basic pattern of past cortisol surges. Once it turns on, you experience changes in your heart rate, digestion, breath, eyes, ears, skin, liver, and reproductive and immune systems. Past experience associated those feelings with threats, regardless of what your verbal brain is thinking. Often, your verbal brain notices the response and tries to explain it with the pathways it has.

You can reroute this response when you understand it. You can accept your natural physical arousal without believing you are actually threatened. You can honor the ancient lineage of your cortisol instead of letting it darken your thoughts and trigger more cortisol.

But you don't feel like doing that while it's happening. That's why it's important to build this skill right now. You can wire in a new approach to cortisol so you will have a new pathway in your brain the next time your senses report a potential threat.

CORTISOL EVOLVED TO PROTECT YOU

Cortisol evolved to protect you from harm in three ways:

1. It commands your attention.
2. It prepares you to act.
3. It wires you to recognize similar future threats.

Let's look closer at these functions.

Cortisol Commands Your Attention

Cortisol grabs your attention even when you'd rather be doing something else. A monkey would rather keep eating when it hears a predator warning from a troop mate. But cortisol makes the monkey feel so bad that stopping it is more desirable than the food. Cortisol feels bad because feeling bad promotes survival. A mammal can survive the loss of a reward better than it can survive a predator attack. Natural selection built a brain that prioritizes cortisol.

Cortisol Prepares You to Act

Cortisol motivates you to do what it takes to make it stop. You don't always know what to do, alas, and you may not even know what "it" is. Maybe a little comment or a tiny facial expression got you started. As much as you don't want to be that kind of person, cortisol keeps trying to protect you from potential harm. It's easy to see why it's called "the stress hormone."

Cortisol prepares you for action by arousing what has come to be called the *sympathetic nervous system*. But in the modern world, physical action is rarely the best response to perceived threats. Thus, we end up squelching our arousal rather than using it. You squelch your arousal when your loved one makes that little comment or your boss makes that tiny facial expression. You squelch the arousal triggered by the electronic images you expose yourself to. But even squelched arousal can give you the sense that something is urgently wrong.

Cortisol Wires You to Recognize Similar Future Threats

Cortisol protects you from future harm by paving neural pathways that turn it on faster the next time. Understanding this function is the key to taming anxiety.

If a toddler touches a hot stove, cortisol paves a pathway that alarms the child the next time it sees a hot stove. Triggering the bad feeling of pain in advance alerts the child in time to act to prevent pain. This works without intellectual knowledge of burns or conscious fear of stoves. All it takes is pain.

In the modern world, we want to prevent pain. We want our kids to learn without having to suffer. Sometimes this works. A parent may tell their child not to touch with enough alarm to trigger the child's sense of pain through its mirror neurons. Gazelles have their own way to do this. A baby gazelle does not understand the threat of predation, but without appropriate caution, its parents' genes would be wiped out. Thus a mother gazelle bites a child that wanders off. The pain of the bite wires the child to release a bad feeling when it starts to wander off. The child sticks close to its mother to relieve the bad feeling.

You got wired by your past pain. You may not remember it because it doesn't require conscious memory to work. It works by building a neural pathway linking a cluster of inputs to the on switch of your cortisol. You didn't have to touch a hot stove twice because cortisol built a pathway the first time. You don't have to remember your first burn for the pathway to do its job.

WHY WE ANTICIPATE PAIN

We anticipate pain in order to prevent it. We can end up anticipating a lot of pain in our quest for survival. No one consciously decides to do this, so it helps to understand the natural mechanism.

A striking example is the girl who had panic attacks when she heard laughter. The girl had been in a car accident that killed her friends. She woke up from a coma to the bad news with no memory of the accident. The crash had triggered a huge cortisol surge, which built huge connections among the neurons active at that moment. She had been laughing in the back seat at that moment, so her brain wired the pain of the crash to the sound of laughter. Her anxiety was her brain's effort to protect her from the anticipated pain.

In the modern world, we see pain as evidence that something has gone wrong, but pain exists because it has survival value. This is easy to see from a reptile's perspective. A lizard spends its whole life running from pain. When it hides under a rock, it feels the pain of hunger and cold, but when it goes out to sun or forage, it risks being eaten alive. It constantly acts to relieve the most urgent threat. When its temperature or blood sugar falls into the danger zone, cortisol motivates it to go out and do what it takes to meet its needs. It's on high alert the whole time, and rushes back into hiding as soon as its urgent needs are met. If it smells a predator, it weighs one anticipated pain against the other. Strategic management theory is not needed to do this. It simply acts on the most active circuit.

When you see a lizard basking in the sun, you may think it's enjoying the good life. You don't realize it's on high alert and struggling to relieve the pain of hypothermia. The lizard doesn't worry about death or the future because it only has enough neurons to anticipate immediate threats.

Fish release cortisol when their oxygen falls into the danger zone. The bad feeling motivates a fish to seek more oxygenated water, and that relieves the cortisol. A plant releases cortisol when it doesn't get enough sun, and that motivates it to grow toward the sun until the cortisol is relieved.

Cortisol motivates action to relieve a threat. But how does a system know when it is threatened?

Nature's Threat Detector

The meerkats at my local zoo go on high alert when a jet flies overhead. You can see them freeze and stare, even though they have never been dive-bombed by commercial aircraft. Some innate pathways must trigger this, since it doesn't fit their lived experience. Meerkats evolved in a world where overhead dark spots swooped down and ate their babies. Their cortisol is triggered by overhead dark spots, even though it's wasted effort for meerkats that live in a zoo near an airport.

Inborn threat circuits make sense. If you had to learn about the pain of a predator's jaws by experiencing it, survival rates would be low. But hardwired pain responses are a problem. They lead to false alarms, and they leave you defenseless against new threats. Natural selection built a brain that can build new pathways from lived experience instead of just relying on pathways shaped by your ancestors' experience.

The bigger a critter's brain, the more it relies on learned pathways rather than inborn pathways. This is clear because small-brained creatures have very short childhoods. The length of a creature's childhood grows with the size of its brain. A lizard has no childhood at all. It runs away from home as soon as it hatches from its shell, and if it doesn't run fast enough, a parent eats it. It manages by relying on inborn survival skills. Survival rates are low when one is only equipped with fixed responses to specific opportunity and threat signals. But enough lizards survive to keep their species alive.

A lizard has very little ability to build new circuits from new experience because it has very few extra neurons. Extra neurons make it harder to survive because they consume so much energy. A critter with extra neurons can only survive by wiring them in ways that more than offset the burden. Wiring neurons from lived experience makes a huge contribution to a critter's ability to meet needs and avoid harm. But it takes time. That's why bigger brained creatures are born with the ability to build survival skills during an early period of dependency rather than with the skills themselves.

Monkeys have a big reserve of extra neurons compared to non-primates. If a little monkey is grabbed from a tree by a hawk, the pain of the claws in its flesh builds a circuit. That circuit includes the sudden darkness created when the hawk's approach blocked out the sun. If the little monkey survives the attack, it will release cortisol as soon as it perceives a sudden darkness. This capacity to anticipate a hawk attack gives it a huge survival advantage. And it works without a cognitive conception of hawks or of danger. Neural pathways do the job.

Your Emergency Broadcast System

Your eyes and ears are constantly flooded with more information than you could possibly process. If you paid attention to everything, you wouldn't notice threats in time to act. Natural selection built a brain that sifts and sorts inputs in a way that zooms in on what's most relevant to your survival. And it does this almost effortlessly.

When your senses are activated by the world around you, they send the particular pattern of electricity to your brain. The electricity flows easily when the pattern has already been experienced, because neurons become more efficient with use. An unfamiliar pattern means trudging down an undeveloped path. The going is so rough that the electricity just peters out sometimes. This is why familiar inputs are so easy to decode that you don't know you're doing it, while unfamiliar inputs send such a weak signal that you tend to ignore it unless a high threshold is reached.

The pain you've already experienced makes it easy to turn on your cortisol when you see something similar. A reward you've already experienced makes it easy to turn on the happy chemicals it triggered. Experience wires you to seek rewards and avoid pain in ways that worked before. Your chemicals make these impulses powerful even if your verbal inner voice does not know the reason for them. You may even deny these motivations with your verbal inner voice. Or you may see them as facts about the world instead of bodily responses created by old neural pathways. You're like the rider who focuses on the trail map instead of on the horse. You can enjoy a better ride through life by getting to know your neurochemical operating system.

Watching animal trainers helps you do this. They have developed the art of building neural pathways intentionally with careful use of rewards. Dolphin trainers are especially interesting because a dolphin is high in the air when it does a beautiful flip, so it's impossible to give an immediate reward. If you reward it when it returns to the water, it doesn't know which behavior is getting rewarded and thus which behavior to repeat. Dolphin trainers started blowing a whistle when the dolphin executed a desired behavior high in the air, thereby training the dolphin to associate the whistle with a fish treat when it gets back to the water. Dolphin trainers "shape" amazingly complex behaviors by rewarding one tiny step after another. Trainers of other animals began using this method with a clicker instead of a whistle, so it has come to be known as *clicker training* or *target training*.

We humans will do flips when we expect rewards. We are always learning about which behaviors get rewarded and which bring pain. We are always building pathways that anticipate future rewards and pain. Your verbal brain rarely understands the sources of this anticipation, but the chemicals are so powerful that you feel motivated with or without your verbal brain's approval. Alas, life is confusing when your verbal brain can't explain your motivations. But you can help your verbal brain understand your mammalian neurochemicals so that your two brains can work together.

Your Danger Radar

The mammal brain is always scanning the world for survival-relevant information. For example, a gazelle doesn't run as soon as it smells a predator because it would die if it ran in the wrong direction. It scans for more information first. It zooms in on details about the location of the threat, and potential paths to escape. It focuses on the path more than on the lion. Its neural pathways do this almost effortlessly.

You are not consciously scanning for information about threats, yet you do it almost effortlessly all the time. You have ten times more neurons going from your brain to your eyes than you have from your eyes to your brain. That means you are ten times more equipped to tell your brain what to look for than you are to interpret whatever just comes along. Your ears work that way too. Your senses constantly scan for information relevant to survival rather than processing whatever just happens to be there. You define survival with pathways built from your past rewards and pain.

Our brain seeks rewards as enthusiastically as it avoids pain because rewards are necessary for survival. But in the state of nature, pain can kill you faster than missing out on rewards, so our brain prioritizes threat signals over reward signals.

If you lived in a world of hunger and predation, those immediate threats would command your attention. But in a world where your immediate needs are met, your danger radar scans out for threats that are more distant in time and space. You can end up with a constant sense of threat even in a life that's quite safe.

SOCIAL PAIN

Social interactions also trigger cortisol. These alarm signals are hard to make sense of because you do not consciously think your survival is threatened when you feel social tension. But the brain you've inherited links social isolation to the jaws of a predator. Social pain hurts because it triggers the anticipation of physical pain.

Of course you don't literally expect to be eaten by predators when you're isolated. But from your moment of birth, you have been building pathways linking the survival threat feeling to social isolation. We are born helpless and vulnerable, needing social support to survive. A lack of social support equals death to an infant. It has no conscious awareness of death, or even of other people, but it's hardwired to release cortisol when it's hungry or cold. That triggers the "do something" feeling, but the infant doesn't know what to do. Social support relieves the bad feeling, which wires the infant to anticipate the relief from social support. Relief doesn't always come, alas, which motivates a child to develop skills for relieving its own pain. But it also wires in life-and-death feelings about social support.

Sometimes social interactions trigger pain rather than relief. Sometimes it's real physical pain, but it's usually just anticipated pain. From a child's perspective, any threat to its social support triggers the anticipation of pain. That wires in the expectation of more pain from similar interactions. Thus we can get wired to expect pain from the very same interactions we seek for support.

Social pain is curiously distressing when other needs are met. When a gazelle is starving, it roams farther afield because the expected reward outweighs the expected threat. But when the gazelle has a full belly, social isolation seems more threatening. It's easy to see how social pain can command your attention. Small threats to your social support can feel like huge threats when they're the only threats you face.

A gazelle can lose its support network at any time if it doesn't notice when the rest of the herd moves on. A brain would have poor survival prospects if it let that happen. Our brain is inherited from ancestors who paid careful attention to what the rest of the herd was doing. A gazelle can't survive by blaming separations on its herd mates. It survives by constantly updating its information on its support network.

Monkeys have bigger brains than gazelles, and more social drama. They groom each others' fur in their free time. Research shows that a baboon's grooming partners tend to come to its aid when it is attacked. You may think of this as heartwarming evidence of cooperation and empathy, but baboons must groom their protectors. They must give "likes" to get "likes." And sometimes these expectations are disappointed. Field research shows that a baboon's distress calls are sometimes ignored by its grooming partners, even when it has risked its life rescuing them. If the baboon lives, it manages this social pain by offering its groomings elsewhere.

We have inherited a brain that promotes survival by anticipating social pain and acting to relieve it. You can create a lot of social pain when you attach a big cortex to a mammalian limbic system. You may interpret your social pain as evidence that something is wrong with the world, or with your life, or with you. It helps to see social pain as information that helped our ancestors survive.

Disappointment

Disappointment hurts because your brain anticipates physical pain. You do not consciously think you're in pain when you fail to get the pony you wanted for Christmas. But cortisol is released when expected rewards don't materialize.

The link between disappointment and physical pain is easy to understand in the state of nature. Imagine you're a lion that hasn't eaten in days. You start chasing a gazelle, but it gets away. Your cortisol surges when you see the growing gap between you and the gazelle. You get a bad feeling about this chase so you stop running. That cortisol saved your life because you would die of starvation if you kept running after gazelles that got away. Disappointment frees you to scan for a more accessible reward.

When an animal fails to find food, low blood sugar triggers cortisol. This sense of urgency could motivate the animal to run after everything, but wasted effort would threaten survival. It needs the information wired in by past disappointments. It takes a really big cortisol blast to get a lion's attention when the cortisol of hunger is already surging. That's why disappointment feels so bad.

We all have limited energy available to meet our survival needs. When you get a good return on your investment of energy, your brain rewards you with happy chemicals. When you get a bad return, it alarms you with cortisol. The bad feeling of disappointment is as essential to nature's steering mechanism as the good feeling of reward.

If you were a hungry monkey, you would want to climb after any piece of fruit you saw. But you might die if you climbed onto a branch that couldn't hold your weight. And you would starve if the fruits you went after were grabbed by other monkeys first. You survive because past disappointments wired you to make careful decisions about which rewards to go after.

We are constantly making decisions about our investment of effort. Past successes and failures wire in expectations about what will succeed and what won't. Past experience is not a perfect guide to how the world works, of course, but it's the guide that is connected to our chemical motivators. Our expectations are disappointed sometimes, but we need expectations to initiate the investment of effort. Our disappointments are easy to remember because big cortisol surges build big pathways.

We learn from rewards and pain throughout life, but the rewards and pain of your youth build the superhighways of your brain, as we'll see in chapter 4. We strive to predict an unpredictable world with a prediction mechanism built in childhood and adolescence. Good predictions about rewards and pain are essential for our well-being. Disappointment feels bad in the moment but it can lead to better predictions.

RELIEF AT LAST

From a survival perspective, relieving a threat is the best reward there is. That's why cortisol commands your attention with the urge to make it stop. It may feel like the world is in crisis when cortisol is doing the job it evolved for.

When you succeed at relieving cortisol, you feel like you've saved your life. Imagine you're a baboon being chased by a lion and you see a tree. Climbing that tree saves your life. The surge of relief wires you to scan for trees the next time a lion threatens. The mammal brain is always scanning for whatever brought relief in its past.

Imagine you are a teenager at a party. You anticipate social disappointments because you have experienced them before. You decide to smoke a cigarette and you suddenly feel less threatened. The relief wires you to expect relief from cigarettes. You don't consciously believe that the cigarette saved your life, but it feels that way to your mammal brain.

Relief feels good because you go back to getting rewards. A gazelle goes back to grazing once it escapes a predator. Anything that shifts you from a bad feeling to a good feeling promotes survival from your mammal brain's perspective. It wires you to seek more relief in that same way.

Sometimes you get relief in ways that harm you in the long run. Then you're in a quandary. You feel threatened when you engage in the harmful behavior, and threatened when you don't. This conundrum is natural. Nothing is wrong with you. Nothing is wrong with the world. You are just a big-brained mammal trying to feel safe in an unpredictable world. You can learn new ways to feel safe. You can trigger the great sense of relief in new ways. You can wire your brain to expect to prevail, the way a gazelle does. Let's see how.

REMEMBER:

1. Anxiety is cortisol triggered by the perception of threat.
2. Cortisol is a full-body sensation that evolved to prepare an animal for action against a threat.
3. Cortisol turns on when a new input activates a pattern of neural pathways paved by past cortisol surges.
4. Cortisol builds neural pathways without conscious intent because that promotes survival.
5. Cortisol gets your attention because that promotes survival.
6. When an organism's survival needs are not met, cortisol alerts it to take action.
7. Neurons consume a lot of energy, so they make it harder for a creature to survive.
8. Creatures with more neurons have a long childhood because it takes a long time to wire neurons in a way that promotes survival.

9. Our brain is constantly learning from rewards and pain.
10. Safety in numbers promotes survival for most mammals, so social support triggers reward chemicals and the lack of it triggers threat chemicals.
11. Disappointment triggers cortisol. An organism has limited energy to get the rewards it needs to survive. When expected rewards do not materialize, cortisol alerts a mammal to the threat of wasted energy.
12. Relieving a perceived threat is a big reward to a brain focused on survival.

3

A TAMING TOOL THAT WORKS

Would my needs be met by raging at the supervisor who gave me a bad review?

Anxiety is a cortisol pathway built from life experience. Fortunately, you can build a new pathway to trigger happy chemicals instead of cortisol. But you have to feed your brain new experiences to do that. This may seem like an impossible paradox. How can you feed your brain new experiences while you're running on old pathways?

The short answer is to focus on what you want rather than what you don't want.

You can't rewire your brain all at once, but you can control your focus for one moment. And you can do it again in the next moment. By carefully planning your focus, repetition will build the new pathway. Your electricity flows more easily each time. This chapter helps you design your new focus, and the following chapters help you find your power to repeat it.

You can design an experience that feels good now and doesn't have bad consequences in the long run. You can design a reliable way to shift into happy chemicals. Wire it in now and it will come more easily in moments of distress.

Maybe you think, "If it were that easy to feel good I would be doing it already." Maybe all your feel-good strategies have bad long-run consequences. But you will learn a new taming tool that leads your inner mammal to natural good feelings.

This taming tool has three steps:

1. Spend one minute asking your inner mammal what it wants.
2. Spend twenty minutes doing an activity you like that completely absorbs you.

3. Spend one minute planning your next step, and take that step by the end of the day.

Practice this taming tool every day and your electricity will flow in a new direction. You will literally forget to be anxious.

This chapter explains the science behind each step so you know why it works. But let's start with some practical examples so you can feel how it works. I'll start with a personal example: the day I got a bad review from my supervisor. I tamed my anxiety with the three-step tool without consciously knowing it!

When I got my review and saw checkmarks in the "fair" boxes, I shook from head to toe. I couldn't wait to run out the door at five o'clock. But I knew I'd still feel awful when I got home to my tiny studio, so I spontaneously decided to walk instead of taking the subway. Walking from Wall Street to Midtown Manhattan seemed like an epic odyssey in 1980, though in the age of digital maps it's clearly just 3.3 miles. In the days before headphones, it felt even longer.

I had been working on Wall Street as a trainee at a bank for a few months. I wasn't really interested in the job, but it was popular at my graduate school, so I gave it a try. Now I seemed to be a wash-out at the mundane tasks they were training me to do.

You may think I wanted to rip the head off of the supervisor who gave me the bad review. But this was not my first workplace setback, so I knew it was more complicated. I had bombed at a few jobs in my twenty-seven years. I grew up in a home with lots of conflict and had learned to avoid conflict by minding my own business. I was good at getting things done on my own, but not especially good at working with others. I wanted to change, but my anxiety surged when I deferred to others. What I really wanted was a job where I got to rely on my own judgment.

I didn't know how to make that happen, but I was out of the banking district and into terra incognita when I had that insight. It was thrilling to see the sights I had ridden under every day. The neighborhoods I was headed toward were not considered safe for a stroll at that time. This gave me a sense of adventure that completely diverted me from my career issues.

Finally I reached the familiar turf of Midtown Manhattan, and my problem drifted back into my awareness. How could I face work the next day? I could smile and try harder, but I would explode if I did that forever. I tried to think of something I could enjoy doing. I had a dream of designing a course. I was already teaching night courses at local universities, but these courses were designed by others. I had lots of ideas for a course of my own. I decided to write a proposal as soon as I got home and find out how to submit it at lunchtime the next day. I felt better as soon as I thought of that. I had the good feeling of stepping toward a goal even though I didn't know exactly what the goal would be. And less than ten years from that moment, I was a tenured professor with significant scope to rely on my own judgment.

Our brain evolved for the job of meeting survival needs. Would my needs be met by raging at the supervisor who gave me a bad review? My brain is designed to make that decision. I made it by quickly defining what I really wanted, taking time to decompress, and then designing a step forward that I could take immediately.

My friend Al used this three-step technique for a different sort of anxiety. Al's lady friend was not returning his calls, and an awful feeling surged through him. The bad feeling turned on whenever he thought of calling her back, or calling another woman, or just using his phone. He was surprised by the intensity of this response, since he had gone through a divorce recently and thought he handled it pretty well. Now, two weeks later, he was suddenly crumbling.

He knew that this lady was not really the issue, because he was lukewarm about her. So he decided to stop and figure out what he really wanted. He had trouble feeling safe with women. When he was young, his mother got sick so he spent time with his grandmother. Then his grandmother got sick. He was mostly on his own then, and he hated to be surprised by things out of his control. He got through the divorce by telling himself he would have more control in his new life. Now he was forced to realize that he wouldn't. Even if he found the perfect relationship, anything could go wrong. He wanted to learn to feel safe in a world he didn't control. He didn't know how to do that, so he went out for a bike ride.

After biking a while, Al stopped for a break. He saw someone pull out a phone and felt a stab of anxiety. It occurred to him that he hadn't felt bad all the time he was on his bike. He realized that he had controlled the feeling even though the world itself was still out of control. Of course he couldn't bike all the time, but he could bike when he needed power over that feeling. He could call a new woman for a date just before his bike ride tomorrow. He might worry until then, alas, so he considered doing it tonight, but that would be a bad time for a bike ride. What if he did it now before his ride home? He pulled out his phone and dialed before a minute had gone by. He couldn't control the world, but he could control where he focused his attention.

STEP ONE: ASK YOURSELF
WHAT YOU WANT FOR ONE MINUTE

Your inner mammal wants to survive. That is not what your conscious brain is thinking, but your conscious brain doesn't control the happy chemicals. If you want to feel good, you have to work with your mammal brain.

Your inner mammal feels safe when it expects your survival needs to be met. Yet you focus on potential threats to meeting needs for most of your day. This triggers threatened feelings even when you do not consciously believe you are threatened. Asking your inner mammal what it wants relieves those threatened feelings by shifting your focus back to what you want instead of what you don't want. Focusing on what you want triggers the expectation of meeting your needs, so your inner mammal feels safe.

You cannot guarantee that your needs will be met, of course. But you can build trust in your ability to meet them. You trust your survival skills to manage whatever comes along.

To be sure your inner mammal gets this comfort, you need to set a timer and spend one full minute clarifying your needs at this moment. But first, you need to know how your inner mammal defines its needs.

Natural selection built a brain that rewards you with a good feeling when you meet a need. The chemicals that make us feel good are the mammal brain's signal that the need is met. The mammal brain does not run on philosophy. It just strives to do things that trigger the happy chemicals: dopamine, serotonin, oxytocin, and endorphin. Each of these chemicals creates a specific good feeling when a specific need is met. You have been feeling them all your life, but you don't know what triggers them. When you know what triggers them in animals, it's easy to see how they work in yourself.

The happy chemicals evolved to do a job. They are not designed to flow all the time for no reason. They are released in short spurts when you take a step toward meeting a need. Each spurt is soon metabolized and you have to take another step to stimulate more of them. These neurochemical facts of life may seem shocking when you are used to thinking of happiness as a right. But when you know how your reward chemicals work, you know that your ups and downs are natural. Instead of feeling threatened by ups and downs, you can feel safe in the knowledge that your brain is doing its job.

You Want Dopamine

Dopamine is the excitement you feel when a reward is at hand. If you were thirsty in the desert, dopamine would surge when you saw an oasis in the distance. Dopamine motivates you to scan for signs of an oasis, and trudge toward it despite your exhaustion.

Dopamine surges in a lion when it sees a gazelle it can catch. The good feeling releases the reserve tank of energy, which gives the lion the energy it needs to prevail.

Dopamine motivates a monkey to crack open a nut, even if it takes hours of trying.

Your dopamine is released when you anticipate a new way to meet a need. It could be the finish line in a marathon or the doorbell of a pizza delivery. You may think these don't meet "real" needs, but once your basic needs are met, your brain keeps looking for new ways to trigger it. Any time you anticipate a reward—perhaps a promotion or the attention of a special someone—you are releasing dopamine. Your brain is always scanning the world for opportunities to meet needs and enjoy the dopamine.

In a world where we have water without trudging to an oasis and nuts without cracking shells, dopamine is a challenge. Our immediate needs are met, so we focus on future needs. Each step toward a future need triggers the good feeling now, whether it's training for a marathon or ordering a pizza.

If you bake a loaf of bread, dopamine surges when you smell it in the oven. Dopamine drove you to shop for the ingredients and knead the dough as well. That first bite of fresh-baked bread thrills you with a huge dopamine surge, but a few minutes later, the need is met and the dopamine stops. Then you have to take a new step toward a new need to get more of it. If you buy bread at a store, you only get a dopamine moment when you cross it off your to-do list. But store-bought bread saves your energy for other ways to stimulate dopamine.

Neurons connect when dopamine flows, which wires your brain to expect more of the good feeling the next time you see something similar. This is how each brain learns when to release it and what rewards to seek. This is how a baby gazelle learns to find food when mother's milk is not enough. Your brain got wired by your past dopamine experiences, whether you remember them or not.

Dopamine is the brain's signal that an investment of effort is likely to be rewarded. Rewards are not always predictable, of course. But if you don't try, you get nothing, so the brain relies on its dopamine pathways to make the best possible prediction. An elephant can only find water in a drought by making a prediction about which path is likely to be rewarded. It relies on the dopamine pathways built by treks that got rewards in the past.

The mammal brain promotes survival by constantly trying to anticipate the best investment of your effort. It releases dopamine when it sees a good opportunity, and the good feeling motivates action. A surge of dopamine gets your attention when you stumble on a good opportunity. We are not meant to release dopamine all the time for no reason. It evolved to promote survival, not to make you happy all the time.

Our ancestors did not have a refrigerator or a pantry. They had to keep finding resources to survive. Dopamine made the endless quest feel good. The good feeling starts as soon as you *anticipate* the reward. The first step of a thousand mile journey triggers dopamine as long as you anticipate a reward at the end. Each step of the journey triggers more dopamine as long as you see yourself getting closer to the reward. A child who decides to become a doctor faces thousands of steps, but dopamine motivates them if the child anticipates a reward. For example, a child who sees a doctor save the life of a relative might enjoy a big dopamine surge that builds big expectations about this particular way to meet survival needs.

A monkey enjoys dopamine when it climbs toward a juicy mango high in a tree. Its dopamine peaks when the mango is within its grasp. That peak dopamine wires the monkey's brain to find reachable mangoes more easily in the future. But the monkey does not expect to feel peak dopamine just from lying around. If it did, it would soon get hungry. That would motivate it to scan for food it can reach. A trickle of dopamine motivates the scanning, and each step closer to a reward triggers more. Monkeys stimulate dopamine by meeting their needs, not by looking for "hacks."

When a reward is more than expected, extra dopamine is released. That builds an extra-large circuit triggering extra-large expectations in the future. For example, if you win at gambling, or taste an amazing new food, or ingest an artificial stimulant, you are enjoying extra-large reward. That wires your brain to seek and find more of the same.

Each of us seeks dopamine with pathways built from our unique individual experience. There are no perfect pathways. No one gets dopamine all the time, but we keep seeking it because our brain evolved to do that.

You Want Oxytocin

Oxytocin is the nice safe feeling of social trust. A gazelle feels safe with its herd because its oxytocin is flowing. A herd is an effective threat detection system. A gazelle can let down its guard a bit when surrounded by others. Oxytocin is the good feeling of lowering your guard in the safety of social support. Even lions seek social alliances, because hyenas steal their kill when they're alone. Elephants need a herd to protect their babies from lions. If they lose a baby, it takes twenty-two months to gestate another, so the survival of their genes depends on social trust in the face of a common enemy.

Today, we have idealized expectations about social support. We like to think gazelles have altruistic feelings toward each other. But in truth, gazelles constantly push their way toward the center of the herd because that lowers predator risk. As they weaken with age, they end up exposed on the fringes, but if they've played their cards right, their genes are already passed on. Herd-following reduces a mammal's chances of being the one that gets eaten. Life in a herd is not all warm and fuzzy, but sticking with the herd improves survival prospects, and oxytocin makes it feel good.

When a gazelle sees greener pasture, it's tempted to wander off. Its needs are easier to meet in a place with less competition from other hooves. But a gazelle's genes get annihilated if it's too independent. Natural selection built a brain that rewards you with a good feeling when you stick with the herd.

A herd only improves your safety if you run when your group mates run. We humans hate the idea of following the herd, but a gazelle that refused to run until it saw the lion for itself would soon be eliminated. Mammals survive by constantly monitoring their group mates and doing what it takes to sustain the bond. Most of the animal noises you hear are the species' way of saying "I'm here. Where are you?" Their herd mates continually respond, "I'm here. Where are you?" If you don't hear the expected response, your cortisol rises. That alerts you to reconnect with your support base, which triggers oxytocin and relieves the cortisol. We have inherited a brain that constantly monitors the availability of social support. We feel curiously threatened without it, even if we're frustrated by the herd when we're with it. Oxytocin rewards you for finding the social trust that promotes survival.

But how?

Neurons connect when oxytocin flows, which wires you to expect that nice feeling when you do things that triggered it before. The sights, sounds, and smells of your oxytocin past turn it on today. Those experiences may have included pain as well, which is why we sometimes seek things that trigger pain. We are all challenged to stimulate oxytocin while avoiding the frustrations of mammalian social groups. Your body quickly metabolizes any oxytocin you manage to stimulate, which is why we seek it again and again. When you understand your natural urge for oxytocin, you can find creative ways to meet this need.

Baboons have big brains compared to gazelles, and they have a big repertoire of oxytocin-stimulating strategies. They groom each other's fur, and the touch triggers oxytocin. That builds trust bonds among individuals who have plenty of conflict in the daily course of meeting their needs. Baboons often cooperate to drive off predators. They even take risks to protect their grooming partners. But research shows that they do this when it benefits their genes in one way or another.

Mammals do not enjoy the kind of all-for-one-and-one-for-all social life that you might wish for. But they keep seeking social support because their brain rewards it with oxytocin.

You Want Serotonin

Serotonin is the good feeling of social importance. Your brain is releasing serotonin when you feel special. You hate to admit that you care about this, but your mammal brain cares about being special as if your life depends on it because in the state of nature, it does. An animal gets more food and mating opportunity when it is more powerful than the individual next to it. That leads to more surviving offspring, and natural selection built a brain that rewards you with the good feeling of serotonin when you have a moment of social power. But the serotonin is soon metabolized, alas, and it takes another moment of social power to trigger more. We mammals strive for social importance because serotonin makes it feel good.

You have probably never heard this view of serotonin or motivation. Nice people don't talk about it or report on the biology. But humans have observed the dominance-seeking behavior of animals for millennia, and ethologists documented it in the twentieth century. They described status-seeking behaviors in animals that are curiously reminiscent of daily life. Animals don't seek status consciously. They simply do what it takes to meet their needs. When an animal sees that it is weaker than the individual next to it, it anticipates pain and restrains its urge to reach for food or a mating opportunity. It must find a safe opportunity to assert in order to survive. Serotonin is the brain's signal that it's safe to assert.

It would be nice to have this feeling all the time, but serotonin evolved to do a job. If you released it all the time, you might assert yourself unwisely and end up worse off. Your brain is designed to reward you with serotonin when you find a position of strength.

You have probably learned that dominance seeking is bad. We are taught to restrain this impulse, and to blame it on "our society." It's hard to think of cute furry animals competing for food and mating opportunity. But whatever you believe consciously, your brain craves serotonin and looks for ways to get it.

Neurons connect when serotonin flows, which wires you to expect it in ways that worked before. Such expectations are often disappointed, alas. Your brilliant contributions often fail to get the response you hoped for. It feels like a survival threat to your mammal brain, even though you are perfectly safe. This is why people invest so much energy in the quest for the next social advantage once their basic needs are met.

Animals seek social power without conscious intent. They just look for ways to feel good and avoid harm. The mammal brain does this by constantly comparing itself to others. When a mammal sees that it's in a position of weakness, cortisol is released and it withdraws to protect itself. When a mammal sees that it's in a position of strength, serotonin is released and it acts to meet its needs. Serotonin is not aggression. It's confidence in your power to meet your needs in a world of rivals.

Serotonin promotes relaxation rather than bullying. Thus, an animal that dominates resources may use them to help others meet their needs. But it keeps trying to stimulate its serotonin too. Its rivals do the same. No mammal has a royal road to serotonin. Each mammal confronts social rivals in each moment.

The mammalian facts of life can be upsetting, but denying them leaves you worse off. You believe that others are trying to dominate you if you can't see your own urge for social dominance. You feel wronged by the one-upping impulses of others when you ignore your own participation in the one-up game.

The mammalian urge for serotonin is hard to satisfy. It may seem like other people get to be special all the time and you are wrongfully deprived. But they face the same dilemma as you, because every mammal brain compares itself to others and feels bad when it sees itself at a disadvantage. You may condemn this impulse in others without realizing that condemning others is a way to put yourself in the one-up position. Moral superiority is the modern way to stimulate serotonin. It's better than violence. But if you are constantly outraged by other people's serotonin-seeking, you end up feeling just as threatened. You can help your inner mammal feel safe by accepting the naturalness of this impulse. You can find ways to make your inner mammal feel special instead of investing in a disappointing quest for the world to make you special.

You Want Endorphin

The word *endorphin* comes from "endogenous morphine." It is your body's natural opioid. Endorphin masks pain with a euphoric feeling. It is only released in response to real physical pain, and it only lasts for a short time.

Endorphin evolved to help an injured animal do what it takes to survive. A gazelle can run with a lion hanging from its flesh because endorphin masks pain. A caveman with a broken leg could seek help thanks to endorphin. You have experienced endorphin if you've ever taken a bad fall and said "I'm fine," only to realize twenty minutes later that you are not fine. Your endorphin masks pain effectively because that's the job it evolved to do.

We are *not* designed to inflict pain on ourselves to enjoy the endorphin. That would be a very bad survival strategy. We are designed to feel pain, after a brief respite, because it gives us the information we need to protect injuries. We can be glad we have endorphin for emergencies instead of trying to chase it.

But people are tempted to chase it. Runner's high is the modern world's best known endorphin stimulator. It's important to know that runners do not enjoy it every time they run. They only get it if they run to the point of pain. Starving yourself to the point of pain triggers it too. The tragedy is that your body adapts, so it takes more and more pain to release it. We are not designed to seek endorphin. We are meant to seek dopamine, serotonin, and oxytocin, and to save endorphin for emergencies.

There are relatively few emergencies in the modern world. We are not bitten by crocodiles when we drink water or by centipedes when we go to bed. We don't starve while waiting for the fall harvest or endure rashes while waiting for spring to make bathing possible. We can eat honey without suffering bee stings. It's easy to forget that endorphin evolved to do a job.

Fortunately, you get a small bit of endorphin when you move your body in new ways. Laughing triggers a bit of endorphin as it jiggles your innards. Exercise triggers a bit of it too. We can be satisfied with small endorphin rewards instead of pursuing big highs with harmful consequences.

The Good Feeling of Getting What You Want

Stop what you're doing and spend one minute asking your inner mammal what it wants. When you understand the happy chemicals, you can define your wants effectively. If you want the seas to part to smooth your way, you will probably not get what you want. If you focus on something you can get, a reward is likely. If you focus on something you can get effortlessly, the reward will be small. Focus on something distant and you will be rewarded for each step toward it.

At first, this focus on your needs can be frustrating because the risk of disappointment is always there. Moreover, you have been taught that it's selfish to focus on yourself and the path to happiness is helping others. But when you ignore your needs, your inner mammal feels like your survival is threatened. Instead, you can zero in on one small need that you can satisfy. Your inner mammal will enjoy the reward, and that will wire it to expect rewards. It will start to feel safer about its needs being met.

You have to define your needs before you can choose the right step. It takes an unmet need to stimulate your dopamine. It takes a new step toward social trust to stimulate oxytocin. It takes a new moment of social importance to stimulate your serotonin. So set your timer for one minute and find out what you most need right now.

You may not feel like doing this in a moment of anxiety. You can only imagine things going wrong. Step Two will help you prevent that. Skip Step Two if it's a real emergency. You know it's a real emergency if your do-something siren blasts and you know exactly what to do. At other times, you don't know what you need, so you rely on old habits that don't really serve you.

STEP TWO: DO SOMETHING YOU LIKE THAT COMPLETELY ABSORBS YOU FOR TWENTY MINUTES

Cortisol has a half-life of twenty minutes. Half of it is eliminated from your system in twenty minutes as long as you don't trigger any more. That can be hard, of course, since cortisol is designed to alert you to danger. You scan for more threat signals, and you are good at finding them when you look. That leads to more cortisol, and you end up in a bad loop. You have to interrupt that impulse in order to flow from a bad feeling to a good feeling.

An activity you love is the way to do it. You may not be in the mood for this activity when anxiety strikes, but each time you do it, you build the path that flows out of your cortisol loop. Each step builds the connections that make it easier the next time. Your brain will start to link the good feeling of the activity to the steps toward meeting your needs.

To make this work, find an activity that

- fully absorbs your mind,
- can be picked up and put down quickly, and
- has no harmful long-term consequences.

Let's take a closer look.

Find a Non-distressing Activity That Fully Engages Your Mind

Maybe you like to walk in the park, but you silently argue with the people who bug you while you walk. Maybe you like to draw, but you harshly criticize your work. Maybe you like video games, but you tense up while you play and end up irritable. Maybe you like yoga, but you think about how hard your life is while you're doing it.

These will not work!

They will lead to more cortisol. You need to truly free yourself from distressing thoughts for twenty minutes. It takes some self-monitoring and experimenting to find an activity that effectively distracts you.

Playing a musical instrument is popular because it absorbs your mind so completely. It's hard to worry and play the guitar at the same time. If you sing while you play, it's even more absorbing. This is just an example—not a suggestion that you take up an instrument. Music is not fun for everyone, so find the activity that's fun for you. Keep experimenting until you find something that absorbs you to the point where you stop thinking about who said what to whom, and who should or shouldn't have done whatever they did or didn't do.

Watching television is popular because it has this effect. There's no judgment here because it's only for twenty minutes. But some alternatives to consider are arts and crafts, playing with a pet or a child, reading something you love, or a form of exercise that you enjoy. Calling a friend or loved one is popular, but you can't control whether the conversation will be uplifting or distressing. Listening to music is popular, but be sure you are not ruminating while you listen. It helps to combine activities, so you fully interrupt your threat circuits and give your cortisol time to metabolize. If you have the time, you can add another twenty minutes so that three-quarters of your cortisol will be gone.

Find an Activity You Can Easily Pick Up and Put Down

My favorite distracter is watching a foreign-language movie while stretching. It absorbs me so completely that I absolutely forget whatever was going on before. You may wonder how this can be done for twenty minutes. It was hard at first, but I soon got to love having this great distracter always waiting for me. I watched a long Spanish soap opera this way.

You may think the activity you love is impossible to pick up or put down conveniently. But you will find a way to adapt it if you try. If you can't bring your guitar to work, find a digital simulator. If you can't indulge in landscape painting, watch a painting lesson or do indoor pastels.

You can call a friend or loved one, but they may not be available to listen to you for twenty minutes. It's important to have an activity you can access reliably.

My reliable distracter when I'm in a public place is to listen to comedy with headphones while walking up and down stairs. I am always ready with comedy recordings that I truly enjoy—not bitter comedy that gets on my nerves. Then when I face a long day of meetings that are less than inspiring, I know I have the power to shift to a new circuit quickly.

If you are enjoying your distracter, you may not want to stop, but you need to move to Step Three to tame your inner mammal.

Find an Activity without Harmful Long-Term Consequences

Life is full of pleasant distractions, but many of them have bad consequences in the long run. When you enjoy such distracters, you also anticipate the harmful consequences and respond with anxiety. Thus, you end up feeling bad when you try to feel good. This conundrum is extremely familiar. You could probably list ten examples in ten seconds and you surely have some favorites. You need a new list of activities that feel good in the short run but don't hurt you in the long run.

At first, you may insist that nothing feels as good as your old reliable habit. But once you account for the anxiety this habit causes you, you will broaden your horizons. You can build your own private collection of healthy distractions. The image of a person knitting at a twelve-step recovery meeting is iconic because it works. If you don't like knitting, open your mind to the universe of other healthy distracters. Experiment with a wide range of options. Try them more than once. Even if it seems impossible at first, you will notice that you start expecting a good feeling when you think of the activity. You can find ways to feel good in the short run without harming yourself in the long run.

It's important to have realistic expectations. You do not need to create a state of euphoria. You do not need to do something "good for you." You only need to distract your mind from thoughts that add fuel to your fire.

Sometimes you can find a way to transform an unhealthy activity into a healthy one. Let's say you love to bake cookies when you start feeling anxious, but you end up eating too much. You can bake healthier cookies and put them into the freezer immediately except for one. Of course it's essential to be honest with yourself when you do this, or you will be back in the muddle of creating pain in your quest for pleasure.

After twenty minutes, your peak cortisol will pass and you will be ready for an action step. If you can continue for another twenty minutes, you will have metabolized three quarters of your cortisol. Then move on to Step Three, because it's essential to tame anxiety.

STEP THREE: PLAN YOUR NEXT STEP FOR ONE MINUTE, AND TAKE IT

You can't relieve all of life's threats in one minute, of course. But doing nothing in the face of cortisol makes you feel like a trapped animal. Finding a step you can take is the key to relieving anxiety.

You may fear taking the wrong step in your rush to choose. We are often warned against acting in haste. But if you had unlimited time, you might never find the "right" step. You feel powerless while you are looking for the perfect solution. Your power lies in your next step, so, focus on that.

A famous producer once said, "If you can't write your idea on the back of my card, you don't have an idea." The same is true for your next step. If you can't formulate it in a minute, you don't have a next step. So spend this time defining the next step you can take toward meeting your needs.

If that step turns out to be too big, you can always break it into two steps. Any challenge can be broken down into chunks that are small enough to act on. You can take the first step toward the first chunk right now. That will put you in a better position to evaluate your next step.

You don't have to complete the step in one minute. You need to choose it in one minute and take it by the end of the day or write a time on your calendar when you will do it. If you feel like you have no options, your next step is to research your options. In one minute, you can write down your research agenda and commit to a time when you will do it.

You will honor this commitment because your horse and rider know they must work together. Have you known people who don't honor their commitment to self? Maybe they expect a lot from others, but they don't expect much from themselves? They neglect their own horse in order to struggle with other people's horses. Their horse feels neglected, and they blame others instead of noticing their own neglect. You have power when you honor your commitments to yourself. Your horse and rider relax because they can trust each other.

You won't find a step that makes everyone happy, or fixes everything for good, but you can get a step closer to meeting a need by the end of the day. No matter what is going on, you can break your needs into chunks that are small enough to manage, and manage the first chunk.

A minute seems short, but you have probably analyzed the dilemma for hours already. More analysis is rarely what you need. If you really do need analysis, commit to doing it. Determine which facts you will gather, how you will evaluate them, and when you will get this done. If you think you are too busy to do this, use the time you would have spent on anxiety.

A gazelle would get eaten if it analyzed its options for too long. Sometimes it can't see the options from where it's standing. It has to start stepping to know the facts. Then it can adjust with corrective steps. Taking steps is nature's cortisol relief.

You may be thinking that a gazelle dies if it chooses wrong. When you think about choosing wrong, you get that feeling of impending doom. A big cortex is designed to anticipate threats. A cortex fueled with cortisol generates a steady stream of disaster scenarios. It's hard to see the rest of the story until you take a step that triggers some happy chemicals. Your first step will trigger some dopamine, and each step toward rewards brings you more. The dopamine will help you scan for positives instead of just scanning for negatives.

A chorus of disapproval may sing in your ear while you're doing this. It feels like other people control the chorus, but you control the microphone. You can grab it back and return the focus to your view of your steps toward your needs. Your critics have their own microphone and their own steps to plan.

You may think you can't step without more money and power. But with more money and power, you'd have more at risk. Every path has risks, but if you choose no path, you just feel surrounded by threat.

So spend a full minute pondering your best next step, and take it. It doesn't matter how small the step is because you can follow it with another step, and another. Every step is valuable. Some steps make visible progress, while other steps just bring you to the point where visible progress is possible.

DIG THE WELL BEFORE YOU NEED THE WATER

You will tame your anxiety if you spend a minute clarifying your needs, twenty minutes lowering your cortisol, and another minute defining a step that's doable. This three-step taming tool may seem awkward and unnatural. You may think you can't do it while anxiety is flowing. But if you do it every day, you will build a new circuit that goes there automatically. Do it now and the circuit will be ready in moments of greatest need. Your investment of twenty-two minutes will add a powerful tool to your tool kit.

Maybe the idea of doing this is raising your cortisol.

- You may fear that you will need endless twenty-two-minute breaks.
- You may fear just thinking about what you want.
- You may fear taking time out to do something you love.

The following chapters help you tailor this taming tool to your unique brain and lifestyle. First, let's take a closer look at why this will work.

REMEMBER:

1. You can build new neural pathways by repeating new experiences.
2. Your mammal brain is focused on survival even though you don't consciously think that. It defines survival with chemicals that tell it when needs are met and threat is relieved.
3. Your brain tends to focus on what you don't want until you consciously focus on what you want. Your inner mammal starts to feel safe when you ask yourself what you want because it starts expecting that your needs will be met.
4. Dopamine is your brain's signal that you have found a way to meet a need. It releases the energy needed to approach the reward.

5. Dopamine triggers the feeling we call "joy" or "excitement" when we anticipate a reward. Each step toward a reward stimulates more dopamine if you perceive that you are closer.

6. Neurons connect when dopamine flows, which turns on the good feeling of anticipation when you see things that triggered your dopamine before.

7. Oxytocin is released when you perceive social trust. The mammal brain rewards you with a good feeling when you find social trust because it promotes survival.

8. Neurons connect when oxytocin flows, which wires a brain to expect more of the good feeling in situations that triggered it before.

9. Serotonin is released when a mammal sees itself in the one-up position. It's not aggression but rather the nice, safe feeling that you can meet your needs in the face of rivals.

10. Neurons connect when serotonin flows, which wires a brain to expect more one-up feelings in situations that triggered them before.

11. Endorphin is released in response to physical pain. It masks pain with a good feeling for a few minutes so you can take steps necessary to promote survival.

12. Cortisol has a half-life of twenty minutes. Your body eliminates it as long as you don't trigger any more. But it's easy to trigger more because cortisol tells your cortex to look for threat signals.

13. To avoid triggering more, find a non-distressing activity that fully engages your mind.

14. Cortisol tells your brain to "do something" to meet a need or avoid harm, so you relieve cortisol when you do something. Just a step toward meeting a need or avoiding harm is enough as long as you have the expectation of further steps.

4

YOUR POWER OVER YOUR BRAIN

A gazelle that smells the flowers may miss the smell of a lion.
We are designed to focus on survival information.

A rider has limited power over their horse, yet a rider can guide a horse to an intended goal. You have limited power over your brain, but you can guide your brain to an intended goal.

A rider often believes they're in charge, so they're surprised when they lose control. Your verbal brain may believe it's in charge, so it's surprised when it loses control of your emotions. Your next step is hard to navigate when this happens. In this chapter you'll find out why your emotions and your verbal brain go in different directions sometimes, and how you can help them work together like a skilled horse and rider.

Our story starts with *myelin*, the substance that turns neural pathways into superhighways. Myelin coats a neuron the way insulation coats a wire, so it conducts electricity up to a hundred times faster than regular neurons. Whatever you do with your myelinated neurons feels natural and easy because electricity flows there so effortlessly.

Myelinated pathways make it easy to walk and talk, as long as you stick to your usual ways of walking and talking. You built those pathways from repeated efforts in youth, though you don't remember doing it. The repeated experience of youth also built myelinated pathways to your cortisol and happy chemicals. These pathways turn on emotions so effortlessly that you don't know how you're doing it. It feels like the world around you is turning on the emotion by presenting threats or rewards.

Myelin is abundant in youth. This abundance allows us to build new pathways without conscious effort. You may have heard the news that neurons build throughout life. The problem is that the new neurons are not connected to anything. It takes a lot of repetition to connect them in adulthood, and even then, you just get tiny new trails. This is why we depend so heavily on the pathways we've myelinated in youth.

You may or may not feel relieved to know that myelin peaks at age two. It remains high until age seven, however. Then it spurts again in puberty. This may seem shocking. Why would a brain that evolved for survival build its superhighways in youth? And how can you redirect your brain when highways built in youth inevitably lead you astray?

This chapter shows you how your autopilot got created, and how you can make adjustments to it. The short answer is simple: you can blaze a new trail in your brain if you get comfortable with the back roads instead of coasting on the highway.

YOUR SUPERPOWER

Imagine you're in the Amazon rainforest and you want to see a special grove of monkeys and orchids. You look at the map and see that the highway doesn't go there. So you set out on a small road, which leads to a smaller trail, which suddenly ends. The only way you can reach your destination is to blaze a new trail. You start slashing at the undergrowth, and tremendous effort is needed just to advance one step. You realize with dismay that the trail will soon grow over so you will have to slash it again on your way back. But you forge ahead, and you're thrilled when you get there—so thrilled that you go back every day. The next day the trail is slightly easier to slash, and in a few weeks, a small path is established. It's not a highway, but it goes to a better place than highways go.

You have the power to reach a better place in your brain if you blaze a new trail through your jungle of neurons. It may not seem like a superpower, but this is the power you have. It's a superpower compared to endlessly following your myelinated roads and blaming others for that choice. Will you embrace this power?

"Hacking" the brain has become a popular topic. Trailblazing is somewhat different. A "hack" is a fast, easy way to change, without all the bother of defining a healthy step and repeating it a lot. If a hack existed, I would have embraced it on page one. You have probably tried a few hacks already. Maybe you're willing to try trailblazing instead.

Many people don't. They have good reasons, according to their verbal brain. Here are some reasons we hear a lot, and how you can overcome them.

1. My Brain Should Be Fixed by an Expert

In today's world, you get the idea that an expert can fix your brain the way they fix your car. You don't mess with the insides of your car, and your brain seems even more daunting.

Your quest for an external fix is disappointed, alas. You have more access to the control panel of your brain than any expert has because you control your thoughts and actions. Your power is limited, but it's more than an outsider has. Your quest for an external fix can distract you from your internal power.

"Getting help" is the solution we hear most about today. The meaning of the word *help* is often misconstrued. Help can assist your steps, but it cannot substitute for your steps. It cannot replace the work you do to install those steps outside of your helping sessions. If you forget that, help doesn't help.

When help doesn't help, you are told that you didn't get "the right help." So you shop for better help. You fight for better help. The fighting, shopping, and blaming consumes energy that could have been invested in trailblazing. Responsible experts know this and encourage you to take internal action instead of just expecting an external fix. But they also want a satisfied customer and a renewal of their license. If you believe in an external fix, and the expert's licensing body does too, the expert must live within those expectations.

The more you believe in an external fix, the harder it is to take internal action.

Internal action is hard anyway, of course. It's scary to leave the comfort of old highways. It's exhausting to struggle with every step. It's tempting to return to the effortless old road, despite its familiar potholes.

Here's a more comfortable way to look at it. Imagine you're riding your horse in a competition. You see other riders who seem to guide their horses effortlessly. You want to be like them. Suddenly, your horse starts bucking out of control. You're so flabbergasted that you want to hand the reins over to someone else. Anyone! But no one has as much control over your horse as you have because you are sitting on it. You want to build your skill at managing the beast, but that's hard to do while it's bucking. And when it stops, you're too tired. But you promise yourself to make it different this time. The next morning you start researching the tools that the other riders use. You discover that they are constantly training with the help of coaches. A few coaches in some cases. You start training too. The competition arrives, your horse bucks, and you look for your coach so you can hand over the reins. But after a few competitions, you realize that your relationship with the horse is what matters. You can manage whatever the horse does, and it feels natural.

2. I Aspire to Something Higher

The word *survival* has gotten a bad image. People tell you to focus on a higher purpose rather than mere survival. That sounds nice, but it doesn't tame your mammal brain. It just leaves you feeling like your survival is threatened when you see an obstacle to your higher purpose. If you think you must perform in Carnegie Hall and rescue orphans from war zones, you end up feeling like your survival is threatened a lot.

When you understand the mammal brain, you know how you construct these feelings instead of seeing them as real threats.

For example, you are taught that serving others is all that matters, so you make it your goal. Serving others is the only socially acceptable way to seek serotonin in the modern world. You feel good when you serve others because it's your chance to feel important. You enjoy dopamine with each step because you anticipate the serotonin reward. You enjoy oxytocin because you feel like you belong when you serve others. You've learned to meet your needs with this service project. And then something goes wrong.

Every threat to your service project threatens the happy chemicals that tell your brain you are safe. If your project loses funding, it feels like a survival threat. Any risk of losing funding is a survival threat. If one person makes one comment that could hurt your funding, your threat chemicals turn on.

Your brain is always focused on meeting your needs. A higher purpose doesn't tame anxiety unless you reassure your inner mammal that your needs will be met.

Many people look to a higher purpose for anxiety relief. When it doesn't work, they make it higher and higher. They end up with great expectations that are often disappointed. Disappointment triggers cortisol, which they interpret as a real threat. You can manage this threatened feeling if you know where it is coming from. And that means admitting that your own rewards are at stake.

3. This Seems Weak

Maybe you see yourself as a conquering hero rather than someone who writes small steps on a calendar. Maybe you want to lead the charge against evil instead of distracting yourself with fun stuff. You want to slay dragons, but without anxiety.

Unfortunately, the brain doesn't work that way. Exposing yourself to danger will turn on your natural alarm system. You have to escape the danger to relieve it. Drowning out the alarm sound with adventure doesn't work. Your alarm keeps blasting until you do something about the danger. So whether you are doing something dangerous or just terrifying yourself with bad thoughts, you need to address the danger at the source instead of just hacking the alarm system.

Strength is a valuable skill on the road to taming anxiety. But it's important to define strength in a way that feels safe. Strong means solving problems. Strong does not mean ignoring problems. If you are ignoring problems, your mammal brain will keep blasting you with a "do something!" feeling.

In the animal world, strong individuals make more surviving copies of their genes, but it doesn't make them happy. They are on the "live fast and die young" track. They face predators and rivals and live with a lot of cortisol between the moments of glory. When they lose their social dominance, they don't last long.

We have inherited a brain that aspires to greatness, but feels alarmed on the path. This paradox is absolutely natural because both feelings promote the survival of your genes.

But we long for a better way. We want to enjoy the great feeling of strength without the bad feeling of threat. This dilemma has plagued humans since the beginning of time. The ancient Greeks addressed it with the fable of the tortoise and the hare. The tortoise seems weak so it's easy for us to identify with the energetic hare. You want to win, but not by being a tortoise.

We take pride in our strength because pride is serotonin. But we define strength with pathways myelinated by the serotonin experiences of youth. Young people take more risks because they have less accumulated experience with threat. When you get older, those risky serotonin strategies trigger anxiety. You need a new serotonin strategy to feel safe, and you need to acknowledge your mammalian urges before you can design it.

WHY THIS WILL WORK

Your power over your brain is limited, so you need to exert it in the right spot to get results. This taming tool helps you leverage your power to redirect electricity from an unhappy pathway to a happier one. You can redirect your horse instead of pretending your verbal brain is in charge.

Your power starts with knowing why your brain doesn't always do what you want. Each brain sees the world through a lens built in youth. You don't consciously decide to use that lens or even remember the experiences that built it. On the contrary, we prefer to think we've left that youthful vulnerability behind and reinvented everything after leaving home. We think we can tame old anxiety by denying that the old lens exists. When you learn to notice it instead, you know it's a pathway built from a random collection of experiences rather than a fact about the world around you.

Your lens is hard to notice because electricity flows into it so effortlessly. You can flow from one automatic response to another without noticing your power to flow in a different direction.

But if you stop what you're doing for a whole minute and ask yourself what you want, your electricity has the chance to find its way into a tiny gully instead of the usual river.

You will not look for the new path if you insist that you don't care about your selfish needs,. That leaves you stuck on the old path because your brain focuses on meeting your needs, whether you think it should or not.

Your old path makes sense when you know how it got there. Three forces are involved: repetition, emotion, and youth.

- Repetition builds a path that you don't notice, the way a fish doesn't notice water.
- Emotion paves a pathway because that's the job it evolved to do.
- Youth paves huge pathways because a young brain is full of myelin.

So whatever happened to you repeatedly, emotionally, in youth built the superhighways of your brain. These highways tell you when to expect rewards and when to expect harm. This is not at all what you are telling yourself with your verbal brain. It's so easy to ignore these pathways that it's essential to know the universals of how they get built.

YOUR LENS ON LIFE

Beneath our individual experience we have a lot of common experience. We are all born powerless. We all feel the pain of gravity when we fall. We all struggle to meet social needs with the equipment we're born with.

A newborn baby knows the pain of hunger before it knows what its mother is, or even what milk is. Low blood sugar triggers cortisol, which triggers crying. That brings relief, which triggers dopamine. Thus a newborn gets wired to expect relief in that way in the future. Soon, it stops crying when it hears footsteps because it anticipates relief—without even knowing what footsteps are. It gradually learns to seek relief by making a noise instead of crying. No conscious thought is necessary. Good feelings wire the brain to expect good feelings from a similar pattern of inputs.

A child's circuits build with each experience of pleasure or pain. These circuits trigger expectations that motivate steps to meet needs and relieve threats. For example, a child's first steps trigger dopamine, not because it intends to walk but because it approaches a reward. Imagine the first time you discovered a way to approach a reward on your own instead of waiting for it to come to you!

Alas, with that joy comes the frustrations of leaving your secure base. Over time, you learn to anticipate the rewards and threats you've experienced. Anything that relieved bad feelings wired you to expect relief in that particular way. The urge to feel good motivates steps that wire in more knowledge about how to feel good.

These pathways fail to bring good feelings sometimes. For example, if a child steals a cookie from another child, it enjoys a moment of social power, but the reward wires in a behavior that hurts in the long run. Many parents say "No, no, no," but they let the child keep the cookie. The young brain learns from the cookie because it is a big reward. You may hate this idea. You may hate people who steal cookies. Yet you may reward bad behavior in this way because you want to be nice.

No one reaches adulthood with a flawless autopilot. The random experiences of youth cannot possibly wire you for every adult eventuality. This is why we resist the idea that our brain is wired by the random chance of early experience. It helps to reexamine it in evolutionary perspective. The larger a species' brain, the longer its childhood. Reptiles have no childhood at all. They run away from home as soon as they're born. A mouse has a month-long childhood, which is infinitely longer. A monkey has a year-long childhood, and an ape is dependent for about four years. From that perspective, a human childhood is extremely long.

A newborn gazelle can run with the herd minutes after it's born. A newborn mouse will be a parent at two months of age and a grandparent at four months. A newborn ape has the power to cling to its mother as she swings through the trees. Humans remain helpless and vulnerable for an extremely long time by contrast.

Being born helpless does not seem like it would promote survival. The longer it takes for a newborn to meet its own needs, the more parental investment is necessary and the fewer offspring its mother can have. Mother reptiles have hundreds of babies and invest little in each one. Mammals cannot do this because a warm-blooded body is so much harder to gestate. So mammals have relatively few offspring and do their darnedest to keep each one alive. They invest their eggs in very few baskets. This further limits their ability to spread their genes. So how do big brains promote survival?

Neurons consume a lot of energy, which makes it harder to survive rather than easier. Extra neurons only promote survival if they're hooked up in a way that brings a big survival bonus. Connecting them from experience is what gives them value. It frees each newborn to learn from its own experience instead of being hardwired with the experience of its ancestors. The more neurons you have, the longer it takes to wire them up in a way that promotes survival.

A reptile can leave home at birth because its neurons are already connected in ways that trigger survival behavior. A mouse needs a couple of months to polish these skills. An ape needs a few years. The bigger the brain, the less wired it is at birth. Our extreme lack of survival skills at birth evolved in a simple way. When our pre-human ancestors managed to find more protein, their fetuses developed bigger brains, which helped them find more protein. This spiral would not work if the fetus's head got too big for the birth canal. So a bigger brain must be born at an earlier stage of development. As brains grew in size, infants got born with fewer circuits but with the ability to build circuits activated by experience. A chimpanzee is born with limbs and senses already hooked up, but a chimpanzee born prematurely looks eerily human except for its small brain.

A species can only survive if each generation learns to meet its own needs before its elders are gone. Children who lose their parents have a very low survival rate in the state of nature. So despite our early vulnerability, we had to wire up as fast as possible. You may think early experience is a bad foundation on which to build a neural network, but that's the system built by millions of years of evolution. You may think of your childhood as inconsequential junk that you have deleted, but you can think of it as an evolutionary marvel instead.

RECOGNIZING YOUR OWN OPERATING SYSTEM

Your core pathways were built in your first seven years of life because that's when myelin is abundant. After age seven, myelin plateaus, which promotes survival in a different way. It's slightly harder for a child to build new branches onto its neural network, which encourages a child to build on the pathways it has. This motivates a child to reference its existing stock of knowledge and locate new inputs in the context of past experience. You can test this for yourself by telling a six-year-old child that the moon is made of green cheese and then telling an eight-year-old. A six-year-old brain is inclined to absorb the information as a fact, while the eight-year-old tends to check it against their stored experience before accepting it as fact. Lower myelin motivates children to add leaves to their neural trees instead of always building new branches. Their brain relates new experience to past experience instead of seeing the world as a newborn each morning. In the state of nature, parents often died young. By age eight, a human child has enough sense to meet its own survival needs in case of emergency.

Myelin spurts again in puberty. This is why the experiences of puberty impact your lens on life so heavily. The myelin of puberty has survival value of a different kind. In the state of nature, mammals leave home at puberty to avoid inbreeding. Animals are not consciously concerned with genetics, of course. They leave their natal group to improve mating opportunity or because they get kicked out. Once they leave, they have to learn new skills to survive in a new setting. The myelin of puberty helps them do that.

An adolescent monkey is terrified when it leaves. We know this from cortisol samples taken in the wild. (In some mammals, all the males leave home at puberty, while in other species, all the females leave). Anything that relieves distress and meets needs builds a pathway that's easily myelinated. What works for you in puberty builds a pathway that wires you to meet your needs in that way in the future.

Throughout human history, people joined new groups or explored new turf around puberty because it improved their mating opportunity. They had to learn new languages, new social norms, and new ways to get home in the dark. When they found rewards or escaped harm, their happy chemicals flowed. Myelin wired them to seek rewards and escape harm in the same ways in the future.

After puberty, myelin dips, and you only have enough to repair the insulation you already built—on a good day. This is why we're all so dependent on our adolescent wiring. It's easy to see this in others. It's harder to see in yourself. You may cringe at the sub-optimality of your adolescence because you are looking at it from the perspective of your adult refinements. We are all in the same boat, trying to meet our needs and feel good with an operating system built in puberty.

Our reactions to the world depend on the circuits we built in youth. Our reactions have a lot in common because our early experiences have a lot in common. When we differ, our own perceptions feel real because real chemicals are being triggered.

The point is not to find fault with your past and your brain. The point is that everyone reaches adulthood with an operating system that needs updates. Your ability to make updates is your superpower.

HOW TO GRASP YOUR BRAIN POWER

It may never feel like the right time to drop what you're doing and face your chemical impulses. One excuse leads to another and the day is gone without spending one minute building your new tame trail. You know you can do it, but somehow you don't. Let's look closer at how we make choices so you can grasp your power to choose differently.

In each moment, we choose between allowing our electricity to flow into our autopilot, or putting on the brakes and finding an alternative path to flow into.

We often jump to the conclusion that the "rational" brain makes the good choices and the mammal brain makes the bad choices. This is simply not true. The fact is that the mammal brain makes all the choices, and the rational brain is simply there to help you define your alternatives instead of whooshing through life on autopilot. This new view of choice is beautifully illustrated by the literary neurologist, Oliver Sacks in *The Man Who Mistook His Wife for a Hat*. He describes a follow-up appointment with a patient who had a severed connection between his limbic system and his cortex. The patient was recuperating nicely and Dr. Sacks asked him to choose the date of his next appointment. The man started debating the pros and cons of alternative dates, but he could not arrive at a conclusion. Dr. Sacks gave him as much time as he wanted to learn about the man's thought process. A long time went by, and the patient simply could not choose. He could skillfully analyze the pros and cons of each alternative date, but he could not generate a subjective preference for one date over another. You may think a preference comes from logic, but it ultimately comes from connecting a positive feeling to one particular option.

Preferences come from your limbic system. You are always responding to information as either "good for me" or "bad for me" by releasing a pleasant or unpleasant chemical. If you want to have a different response to the world, you need to change the pathways that turn on your chemicals. For example, if you want to quit smoking, attach a positive feeling to an alternative self-soothing strategy. That will work much better than the usual approach of using logic to terrorize yourself about the consequences of smoking.

We have two brains because we need both. The cortex is good at gathering detail, but you only draw conclusions from the detail by releasing a chemical that says "this is good for you, go toward it," or "this is bad for you, avoid it." You may think your conclusion came from logic because your mammal brain doesn't talk to you in words. You think your verbal inner voice is the whole story. But your mammal brain literally connects your cortex to your body. You need it to act.

You will not tame anxiety by squashing your mammal brain with the power of your intelligence. You tame it by redirecting your mammal brain onto a new path. This seems hard because the moment of choice passes so quickly. You make thousands of tiny decisions each day without noticing them. You can choose the road less traveled in your brain if you build your power to stop at the moment of choice to give yourself time to notice alternative paths.

Even a goat can do this. I saw it myself in a clicker training class that I took as a zoo docent. A goat was being trained to walk across a see saw to get a reward. The goat rushed to the top of the see saw, but it froze in terror as soon as it felt the shake at the fulcrum. I froze too as I looked into its eyes. Suddenly, the goat burst into action and walked down toward the expected reward. Then it quickly climbed back up to get another reward, and crested without the hesitation this time. I was thrilled to have such an up-close and personal look at a mammal brain conquering anxiety and building new skills.

The better we understand that moment of choice, the more power we have over it. So let's zoom in and take a closer look.

When an ocean liner changes course, no turn is visible for twenty minutes. It takes a huge investment of energy to turn a ship. Imagine investing all that energy without seeing a result for twenty minutes. If sailors limited themselves to actions that got immediate results, ships would never turn. Navigation is possible because sailors trust their skills and wait for their efforts to take effect.

It's the same way with your brain. You may not feel a dramatic change in the moment when you stop and change course. The results will become visible later, but only if you invest the effort now.

So how do you master that moment of course correction?

YOUR PEAK POWER

You have the power to redirect your electricity. You have done it many times, but you don't know how you do it. Let's look closer at this power so you can use it to tame anxiety.

Your senses are constantly taking in information from the world around you and sending patterns of electricity to your brain. Those patterns depend partly on the facts of the world and partly on the neural pathways you receive them with. When the world fits your template, electricity flows easily.

Sometimes, the world doesn't fit. Then you have a choice. You can "go with the flow," and let your electricity move into the best available match. Or you can stop the action and reexamine the pattern that is actually triggered. For example, if you see a movie marquis that says, "Star Wa2s," you could interpret that as "Star Wars," or look for a meaning for the details actually reaching your eyes. In this case, defaulting to the familiar pattern seems so reasonable that you barely notice the difference between the actual input and the old pathway. But if you are on a country road at night and one light is coming toward you, jumping to conclusions is dangerous, so you stop to consider alternative possibilities.

All day every day, you are matching incoming patterns to the patterns you stored from past experience. Life is easy when you decide that a new input fits an old template. You feel like you know what is going on. This is why we rely on old pathways even when they make us feel threatened.

Why is it so hard to take a closer look instead of defaulting to your automatic impulse? To answer this we have to zoom in even closer. Neurons do not literally connect. There is always a gap or *synapse* between one neuron and the next. Your electricity can only flow if it has enough power to jump across the synapse. That's easy for myelinated pathways. It's easy for inputs that are big and loud. And it's easy for synapses that have already seen a lot of action. Experienced synapses can ferry electricity more efficiently. It's as if they have more rowboats ready to transport an electrical charge to the other side.

Without these advantages, an electrical signal may fail to jump across the synapse, and you lose the information. Sometimes that's good. You don't want to waste attention on every detail around you. Ignoring the irrelevant helps you interpret the relevant. This is how our brain is designed to work. But it's also why we tend to ignore things we're not already wired to notice. We feel safer on the trails that are well-stocked with rowboats.

Fortunately, you add new rowboats to your fleet when you repeat a new thought or behavior. Your brain adds new receptors to your synapses when you use them a lot. That makes it easier to notice the information you used to overlook. But those receptors disappear if you don't use them. In short, your brain molds itself to the inputs you feed it. If you feed it a lot of positive inputs, it becomes more skilled at processing positive information. If you don't, positive information is easy to ignore.

If you feed your brain with a diet of negative information, you are very good at processing that. This is natural. We are designed to focus on survival information. A gazelle that smells the flowers may miss the smell of a lion. So don't be too hard on yourself when you fear leaving those old roads. But you can become the superhero of your own life by leaving the anxiety road and blazing a new trail.

It's easier when you plan the new trail because reusing a path develops it faster. For example, if you want to quit smoking, plan an alternative self-soothing strategy instead of focusing on what you are giving up. Each time you feel the urge for comfort, focus on the new choice and the synapses will soon have more rowboats. Your electricity will start to flow and it will soon feel natural.

Your power lies in the instant when you stop coasting and choose a new trail. This is a rather limited kind of power. It would be nicer if you had the power to move the highway so you could keep coasting. But you don't and you can't, so you can either embrace the power you have, or be powerless.

It's easier to seize that moment when you expect to get a reward. The goat at my zoo expected raisins, which are very rewarding to an animal designed to eat grass. In the long run that sugar would be unhealthy, but goats have no long-run access to raisins. Humans, by contrast, have access to unnaturally large rewards every day of our lives. Such rewards bring added risk, which adds to your anxiety. Let's see how you can design a self-soothing strategy based on healthy rewards.

REMEMBER:

1. Myelin is a substance that coats neurons, turning them into super-efficient conductors of electricity.
2. Whatever you do with your myelinated neurons feels natural and easy because electricity flows there so easily.
3. Myelin is abundant before age eight and during puberty.

4. We can build new neural pathways in adulthood, but it takes a lot of repetition. And it takes a big investment of energy to send electricity down an unmyelinated pathway.

5. Our brains wire from experience. The rewards and pain of youth built the pathways that tell you where to expect rewards and pain today.

6. The bigger an animal's brain, the less it is wired at birth, and the more its wiring is built from experience. We humans are extremely helpless and vulnerable at birth, and take a comparatively long time to build our core neural networks.

7. Your cortex and your mammal brain are designed to work together. Your cortex cannot make decisions. It can arrange data in different ways, but no decision is made until your mammal brain releases a chemical that tags an option as good for you or bad for you.

8. Your cortex has the power to redirect your electricity from the path of least resistance to a new path of its choosing. But it takes a big investment of energy.

9. Each time a neural pathway is activated, it flows more easily, though far less easily than a myelinated pathway.

5

DESIGN THE TOOL
THAT'S RIGHT FOR YOU

You can construct the good feeling of approaching rewards instead of waiting for rainbows to find you.

There is no one right way to tame anxiety because each brain is built from life experience. You can design the anxiety-taming circuit that works for your unique collection of happy and unhappy pathways. This chapter shows you how.

1. You will learn to define what you want in a way that motivates your mammal brain as well as your verbal brain.
2. You will learn to distract your inner mammal from threat signals in healthy ways.
3. You will learn to take a step that triggers happy chemicals and wires in the expectation of feeling safe.

You may think it will be hard—even impossible—to steer your inner mammal toward these new steps. This chapter concludes with a practical guide to using carrots and sticks to steer your inner mammal. We are all familiar with the concept of motivating horses with carrots and sticks, but most of us shy away from using this powerful tool. Your verbal brain shuns it, insisting that you don't care about carrots and you're too peace-loving to use a stick. These illusions deprive you of your most powerful tool for managing your inner mammal. You can harness the power of rewards and pain to train your two brains to cooperate instead of going in different directions.

STEP ONE: DEFINE WHAT YOU
WANT IN A WAY THAT MOTIVATES YOUR
MAMMAL BRAIN AS WELL AS YOUR VERBAL BRAIN

Set your timer for one minute and ask yourself what you want in this moment. It may feel awful at first as your mind floods with past disappointments and anticipated future disappointments. Your desires may seem out of reach. But if you stick with it for a whole minute, you can target your greatest unmet need in this moment, and define it in a way you can actually step toward.

Listening to your needs helps you feel safe because neglect of your needs makes you feel threatened. You may have been taught to focus on the needs of others and deny your own. Or you may have learned to expect others to meet your needs, and now you feel powerless to do it yourself. These beliefs tell your inner mammal that its needs will not be met, which feels like a survival threat. You may not know where that threatened feeling is coming from, but when you listen to your needs, your inner mammal feels relief.

What if you want something harmful or out of reach? You don't have to go there because you know what your inner mammal really wants: dopamine, oxytocin, and serotonin. You can design practical steps to stimulate them. You can construct the good feeling of approaching rewards instead of waiting for rainbows to find you.

Your brain defines "rewards" as anything that meets a need. It knows that a need has been met when a happy chemical is released. But old pathways control the happy chemicals, and that limits your expectations about rewards. You can access a new universe of rewards by building new pathways. New oxytocin can be stimulated by creating moments of social trust. New serotonin can be stimulated by seeing yourself in a position of strength. New dopamine can be stimulated by stepping toward a new way to meet a need. Here are some examples.

To spark serotonin, give yourself permission to take pride in something you've done. You may think it's wrong to applaud yourself. You may crave the applause of others. But if you wait for the world to applaud you, you may never take a step. Instead, you can be impressed with yourself for a minute a day instead of always being impressed with others. That will build the pathway to turn on the good feeling more easily. You may be very critical of yourself, but you can praise yourself once a day. And don't ruin the pleasure by resenting others for failing to see your brilliance. Just take a step you can be proud of and feel good about it. A good feeling today is worth more than grandiose illusions about the future. You can train your inner mammal to feel safe with tiny moments of power that you can repeat.

To spark oxytocin, create a moment of reciprocal trust. Give and receive support for one moment. Make careful decisions about which support meets your needs instead of grasping at any enmeshment available. You can start by either offering support to someone else or noticing the support that someone offers you. Make an effort to close the loop by accepting goodwill after you offer it, or returning the goodwill you receive. Then be satisfied. A moment of reciprocal trust triggers that good feeling of oxytocin and builds the pathway. Don't ruin it by expecting endless all-embracing support. It's natural to want that because the vulnerability of youth is the foundational circuit in your brain. That urge motivates the quest for oxytocin, but it can also lead to disappointment. Instead of condemning the world for inadequate support, enjoy tiny moments again and again.

To spark dopamine, find a new way to step toward an unmet need. Find a goal you can actually step toward rather than a dream that is always out of reach. You need to see yourself approaching a reward to stimulate dopamine. For example, if you hate your job, an approachable goal would be to shift 20 percent of your workday into a project you find more interesting. You may need a new skill to get such a project, and you can start building that skill today. If you dream of being rich instead, you may get a moment of dopamine, but it stops when the progress stops.

You may think you don't have the time, money, or peace of mind for this. But when you define a step that's small enough, a good feeling starts now, and that helps illuminate another do-able step. The regular flow of good feelings trains your brain to expect good feelings by finding the step you can take.

Does it feel dangerous to want something? You may have gotten wired to think you are bad if you want something. Or that everything will go wrong if you want something. Or that you will always be disappointed if you want something. You may even pride yourself on not wanting anything for yourself. You can get an "A" in Philosophy 101 with that strategy, but it leaves your mammal brain feeling threatened. Wanting and seeking is the job your brain is designed to do. It's the job happy chemicals are designed to reward. You may get disappointed when you want and seek, but in the long run you will enjoy more happy chemicals.

The clock is ticking. Don't wait for the wind to carry you. Define your needs in the next sixty seconds.

Jan's Story

Let's see how a woman named Jan used this tool. Jan was gripped by anxiety about her daughter. She wanted her child to be happy, but things never seemed to work out that way. Recently, Jan's daughter was left out of a party that her friends were invited to. The news upset Jan tremendously. She was surprised at her reaction but couldn't stop herself from feeling her daughter's pain over and over. She realized she needed to do something so she set a timer for one minute and asked herself what she wanted.

She wanted her daughter to be happy, of course. She didn't want her daughter to suffer the way she suffered. The memory of her own suffering was dim. She liked to think she was past all that. She couldn't believe that her anxiety was just old pain in new bottles. She hated the way her mother wallowed in old pain when she was young. It felt like she was surrounded by her mother's pain all the time. Suddenly she realized with horror that she was surrounding her daughter with her own pain. This is not what she wanted at all. Good intentions didn't make it good. She urgently wanted to give her daughter a happy model rather than the unhappy model that she had. Jan had no idea how to do that since she wasn't feeling happy and sort of dismissed happiness as selfish and disloyal. But she knew it was precisely what she wanted.

Joe's Story

Joe feels anxious at work. He hates the politics. Everything seems unfair. He starts feeling bad about work before he arrives in the morning and he keeps feeling bad about it when he goes home at night. Joe is tired of feeling bad and decides to do something. He sets his timer for sixty seconds and asks himself what he wants.

He wants those idiots to grow up, of course. Why can't they just obey the rules and do their share? He had this problem growing up and he's tired of it. His brother was always breaking the rules and leaving the consequences to others. Joe often picked up the pieces—partly to do the right thing and partly to avoid getting punched. It made him so mad. Now he steers clear of his brother's tornado, so he thought the bad times were over. But these jerks at work are doing the same thing to him. Suddenly Joe realizes that he is doing the same thing as well. He is cleaning up other people's messes to avoid getting punched. He doesn't want to do that. Suddenly he knows what he wants: to stop being the fix-it guy for other people. But if he's not the fix-it guy, who is he? He doesn't know, but he's determined to figure it out.

STEP TWO: DISTRACT YOUR INNER MAMMAL FROM THREAT SIGNALS IN HEALTHY WAYS

Set a timer for twenty minutes and do something you like that fully absorbs your mind.

Your body will eliminate half of its cortisol in twenty minutes as long as you don't release more. It's natural to release more, alas, because cortisol tells your cortex to find threats. To prevent a cortisol spiral, engage your brain with something you like.

When cortisol is flowing, you see the worst in everything. If you try to plan your next step at this time, you will only see the bad. But after twenty to forty minutes of distraction, you can be open to a wider range of possibility.

Distraction has a bad image because it can be misused. But it can also be a valuable skill. You can tame anxiety when you can shift your attention from threatening to unthreatening pathways. Daily practice makes it easier to do that in a moment of distress. Practice staying positive for a whole twenty minutes.

Let's say you love to play the saxophone, but you get distressed over a wrong note. You love private time with a special someone, but you worry about their displeasure. You love cooking, but you overeat. Anything you love comes with the risk of frustration. But with practice, you can stay in a neutral or positive mind-set for twenty minutes. You can't force yourself to be happy, but you can force yourself to focus on something other than potential threats. If one activity isn't working for you, shift to another—even during the twenty minutes.

Maybe you're already a world-class distracter. In that case, be sure to limit your distraction time to forty minutes. This time is your reward for Step One and your preparation for Step Three—the important challenge of facing your true desires and shifting into action.

Unhealthy distracters are all around us. "Everything I like is illegal, immoral, or fattening" goes the old saying. Healthy distracters are everywhere too. You may not notice them because they must be cultivated. The difference between immediate pleasures and cultivated pleasures is neural pathways built from experience. Immediate pleasures are biological while cultivated pleasures are learned. Biological pleasures have consequences.

They evolved because of their consequences. Anxiety often results from these consequences. You're in a mess if you can only feel good from activities that lead to feeling bad. Cultivated pleasures are the answer. Find an activity you like and invest twenty minutes a day. The goal is not to be "good at it." The goal is to be fully absorbed in it, so your mind is not looking for threats.

With repetition, you will build a happy circuit that's big enough to compete with your unhappy circuits.

When you see other people enjoying cultivated pleasures, you may think they were born that way. In fact, they are activating circuits built from repetition. Do not feel left out when you see someone making music or baking a cake or building a robot. Just find something that appeals to you and invest twenty minutes.

Start by listing the activities you already love and wish you had more time for. Then cross off the ones that are inaccessible or bad for you. Now think about new activities you might add to the list. Chapter 7 is full of suggestions for engaging distracters.

It helps to recognize the dopamine, serotonin, and oxytocin aspects of possible choices. Oxytocin is stimulated by social activities as you build trust and anticipate support. Serotonin is stimulated when an activity builds pride in your skill. Dopamine is stimulated when you seek and find, which includes athletic goals, creating things, collecting things, and learning things. Music stimulates dopamine because your brain anticipates patterns and then seeks and finds patterns that confirm its expectations.

This is not the time for things on your "good for you" list. It's not for sit-ups or steaming broccoli, or cleaning closets unless you actually like that. You need to give yourself twenty minutes of something you like to build your anxiety-taming circuit.

Find a way to make your activity accessible in small chunks of time. You may think it's impossible, but you will find a way. You can assemble a painting kit that's small enough to use at work. You can research your dream trip to the Galapagos Islands without spending money. You can use headphones to play an electric keyboard while your baby is napping. You can read recipes and plan your next gourmet dinner. I have even learned to watch movies in twenty-minute chunks. As much as I hate to stop after twenty minutes, I love having something fabulous to go back to the next time I need a lift.

Double-check that the activity meets these anxiety-taming needs:

- you don't brood about threats while you're doing it because your mind is busy;
- there are no harmful long-term consequences;
- you enjoy it, despite occasional frustration.

It's best to have more than one of these activities. Then you will always be prepared with an alternative when one activity is not accessible or stops exciting you. Imagine stocking a whole pantry full of activities you enjoy!

Jan's Story

Jan thinks she's far too busy to spend twenty minutes on something fun. And with all her stress, she can hardly imagine something fun. She struggles to remember the last time she had fun. She pulls out her photos to help her remember. It reminds her how much she likes taking pictures and how proud she is of some of them. She has always wanted to do something with them. She could make something beautiful if she had the time. Suddenly, she realizes that she could give herself twenty minutes right now. It's not a lot, but refining her photos for twenty minutes a day would be more fun than waiting for a day of unlimited time that may never come. She would love to spend a few minutes each day molding her photos in the way she's always dreamed of, and this is something she can actually have. She would have wasted the time on anxiety anyway, she realizes.

Joe's Story

Joe is eager to take his cortisol-relieving break and knows exactly what he wants to do. He will make a lasagna. He has always wanted to make some of the cool things he sees on cooking shows. He can't make a lasagna every day, of course, but he also wants to make the moussaka he saw, and the cheesecake, and probably all five of the cheesecakes. He has thought of a way to make this practical. He will do the prep one day and the assembly the next day. Instead of overeating, he will cut it into modest daily portions and freeze whatever he doesn't give away. He knows his diet will actually improve because fresh, healthy ingredients will replace processed food. His friends groan when he talks about cooking, but he knows they'll change their minds when he hands them a slice of cheesecake. And he doesn't really care because he is so glad to be doing instead of watching.

STEP THREE: TAKE A STEP THAT
TRIGGERS HAPPY CHEMICALS TO WIRE
IN THE EXPECTATION OF FEELING SAFE

Set a timer for one minute and zero in on a step you can take right now.

You may think there are no possible steps. You may insist that you have done everything and now it's up to others. When you believe this, you are like a trapped animal with no options. Anxiety results.

When cortisol says "do something!" you have to find something to do. Your next step is your power. The step may feel risky for a moment, but doing nothing feels more threatening in the long run. Here's how to get into gear.

1. Define Goals You Can Step Toward

Dopamine is released when you see yourself one step closer to a reward. Of course you can't guarantee progress toward your goal, so it's useful to give yourself three goals—a short-run goal, a long-run goal, and a middle-term goal. Then you can always shift between goals when one seems stuck. You can always be stimulating the joy of dopamine.

It's important to remember that progress is not always visible. Most human achievements came from efforts that did not get immediate visible rewards. This makes life complicated. It's hard to keep investing in steps that do not make visible progress. Disappointment wires you to expect more disappointment. What keeps you going is the expectation of reward. How do you sustain this expectation without immediate rewards?

Old dopamine circuits do the job. A person who invests tirelessly in a goal was somehow rewarded for that activity as a child or adolescent when myelin was abundant. Research the childhoods of famous people and you will see where their expectations came from. So where does that leave you today? What if you focused on becoming a rock star or a brain surgeon and only got disappointment? What is your next step from there?

Consider the animal perspective. An elephant may have to walk fifty miles to find water in a drought. It takes a big risk when it chooses its first step. The choice comes from neural pathways built by past successes. With every step, the elephant scans for patterns of sights, smells and sounds that match past successes. The great dopamine feeling of being on the right track is triggered by those matches. But there is no actual track—there is only that trickle of dopamine. Sometimes the elephant is on the wrong track. Then it has to start over, exhausted and dehydrated. It goes back to scanning the world for patterns that match past experience. Giving up is not an option. Choosing its best next step is the survival tool it has.

The truth about elephants is more complicated. Female elephants stick with a herd to protect their young from predators. They line up in strict age order and follow the steps chosen by the eldest. A female elephant does not choose her steps until everyone in front of her is dead. This illuminates the paradox of human choice. We get upset when we have to follow and we're quick to criticize the choices of anyone in a leadership position. But when we have to choose our own steps, we get upset about that too. We get water so easily that we have energy to waste on this kind of lose-lose thinking. But you can enjoy a win-win feeling instead if you celebrate your power to step and also celebrate the help of those in front of you.

We all fear stepping in the wrong direction. But every great success in history has come after multiple failures. We would not have flush toilets or adequate food if our ancestors limited themselves to steps that got immediate visible rewards. We are designed to build a path in our mind instead of just relying on paths that already exist. You can develop a clear mental image of the path you need, and keep scanning for clues to your best next step. Your dopamine circuits will build.

Define your goal in a way you have control over. For example, if your goal is to have a loving partner, you cannot control the love of others. Many people fail to take steps as a result. They just wait for Cupid's arrow to find them. Instead, you can identify steps toward that goal that are within your power. You can invest a set amount of time every day building relationship skills and dating purposefully. You can meet that goal every day regardless of what others do. You can enjoy the good feeling of approaching a goal instead of wallowing in cortisol.

Goals involving weight and finances also trigger widespread frustration. Many people lack energy for other goals because they've spent it all on body and/or money goals that never feel rewarding. You can escape this trap by introducing a new short-term goal that gives you a sense of accomplishment. You can conquer the technology that drives you crazy or make peace with the person who gets on your nerves. You can set a goal of relieving an irritant that bugs you each day instead of focusing on grandiose abstractions that never reward you. You can produce good feelings regardless of your current weight or financial position.

Sometimes I feel bad about a need I've failed to meet. But when I stop to think about it, I see that I haven't invested much in seeking it because I was focused on other things. Usually there's a good reason. We all have limited energy. So instead of dwelling on disappointment, I focus on my power to meet a need when I choose to make it my priority. Until then, my brain will make social comparisons because I'm a mammal. But I can stop myself from spewing cortisol over the rewards of others by focusing on my own steps. (More on social comparison in chapter 8 on pitfalls.)

2. Celebrate the Power of Small Steps

Big steps are exciting, so they attract your attention. You see a lot of big steps in the movies so they come easily to mind. Small steps may seem worthless or boring. In the real world, grand steps rarely happen, but small steps can happen all the time. Small steps are the power you have.

Watch a video of a mountain goat climbing a cliff. It's hard to believe a sheer cliff can be climbed, but the goat does it with grace and speed. It doesn't do it by focusing on the mountain, but by scanning for its next tiny foothold.

Small steps work when you commit to repeating them. I conquered my clutter in small steps because I kept stepping until the job was done. If you dream of a new life, define a path that can lead there and take the first step. You will climb your mountain in steps that are small enough to take.

Small steps are frustrating if you are focused on the mountain. Frustration wastes energy that could be invested in action. Once you see the path, small steps feel rewarding rather than frustrating. Often, you can't see the path until you take a few steps. You have to accumulate information to uncover possibilities. Thus, those first few steps must be taken into the unknown. You may hate to take steps unless you "know what you're doing." This leaves you stuck. It's easier to step into the unknown when you see it as a trailblazing mission. Sometimes those first steps help you see that your mission is impossible. That frees you to find a better place to invest your energy.

You may be waiting for a big dramatic opportunity to appear. You may expect the world to change in a way that suddenly gives you what you want. Life can pass you by while you're waiting. You are better off defining practical steps that lead toward your desires, and taking the first step today.

3. Focus on Your Own Steps

When you dream of something you want, you may quickly think of what other people should do to help you get it. Advice mongers even tell you that getting help is your first step. This strategy often fails because others are not as invested in your goal as you are. Your steps are what you have power over. Don't waste it waiting for others to blaze your trail for you. Once you are on the path, you can find people whose paths overlap.

If you look for a cheering squad, you may not find it. You may waste your energy critiquing others instead of bolstering your own steps. This unfortunate choice is extremely common. The cortisol of disappointment sends your mind looking for evidence that others have let you down, and you are good at finding it when you look. You enjoy some serotonin when you berate their inferior ethics. You enjoy some dopamine when you make predictions and confirm them. You enjoy oxytocin when you bond with other people who feel shortchanged. But the victim template terrorizes your inner mammal. You are like a rider who ignores their own horse to focus on some other horse. Your horse starts to balk.

When I'm disappointed by others, I focus on something I have control over. I define my goal in a way that can be reached regardless of what any one person does. I don't make someone else the gatekeeper of my happiness. And if I've already done that somehow, I uninstall them. If someone gets on my nerves, I tell myself that it's my nerves, which I have power over. I set a goal of not being triggered by them. I visualize my path as something I am choosing with each step instead of something "they" are forcing onto me.

It's natural to want support, but it's also natural for others to be focused on their own goals. You don't have to see their lack of support as an obstacle. You don't need the world's approval to prioritize your goal. You can remain open to others without being dependent on their support. You can learn from their reactions and build reciprocal alliances. You can avoid disappointment if you remind yourself that other people are mammals and you are a mammal too. They see your steps through the lens of their own needs. You are doing the same, even if you don't intend to. Maybe you can cooperate and meet your needs with combined efforts. Maybe not. You will know when you spend a minute clarifying your next step.

Of course there are steps you can't take without support. But you can define them in ways you have power over. Instead of waiting for the phone to ring, you can define the outreach efforts you will make each day. When you reach that goal, you can feel rewards whether or not you get a "yes" on that day. Define a next step that you can take without support. Then you can access the joy of moving forward instead of always feeling threatened by obstructions. Support will trickle in while you are busy taking steps.

Mammals need social alliances to survive, but we are tempted to idealize these alliances. You might think the right allies would make your climb easy. It helps to remind yourself that mammalian social bonds are built on reciprocity. Two monkeys cooperate to beat a common enemy and then revert to competing when they prevail. Do not expect idealized support and end up with nothing. Build trust in small reciprocal steps.

Jan's Story

Jan wants to set a happy example for her daughter, but she doesn't know how. She can't see how she will figure it out in sixty seconds. Then she remembers that she only has to choose her next step. She tries to think of a step toward dopamine, oxytocin, or serotonin. It feels strange since she's not used to thinking about her life in that way. She doesn't know anyone who thinks this way. She imagines the criticism she would get if she tried to explain this to people she knows. Suddenly, she notices her pattern. She is always imagining people criticizing her. What if she did the opposite? What if she imagined people supporting her instead of criticizing her? It would be risky. They might shoot her down and the disappointment would feel worse than ever. It would only be one disappointment if she only tried it once, but it would feel like a bad omen. Now she sees that she just repeated the pattern of anticipating failure once again! Expecting criticism comes effortlessly, while expecting support is something she's not sure how to do. Then she realizes that expecting support for one moment would be a valuable step forward. She could call one person and expect that person's support, and it wouldn't matter if she got it or not because she will have already benefitted by the act of expecting it. So with the clock ticking, she calls her biggest imagined critic, and while the phone is ringing, she imagines the fun of sharing her new knowledge of the mammal brain. She feels like someone will be interested, so if it's not this person she will try someone else tomorrow.

Joe's Story

Joe feels stuck. It seems like the jerks at work will always be jerks, so why would he think it could be different. Only fifty seconds left. This is ridiculous. He can practically feel the punches he would get if he tried to change things. Then he realizes that he created the feeling of being punched with his imagination. He decides it doesn't matter because they really would hurt him if he stopped submitting to their BS. Forty seconds left. Joe's mind goes back to the cruel vengeance he anticipates, and his desperate urge to avoid it. He sees how he imagines a world full of predators. He spends most of his energy running from these predators. What if he took one step toward a greener pasture instead? What if he worked on the new project he loves instead of putting out fires. He reaches for the new-project file and lays it on top of the cleaning-up-their-mess project. His fear of predators surges immediately, and he almost changes his mind. But the thought of the new project feels so good that he decides to take the risk. He will trust himself to deal with potential threats if and when they actually appear.

MANAGING YOUR BRAIN WITH CARROTS AND STICKS

Your inner mammal is motivated by rewards and pain, even though your verbal brain won't admit it. The skillful use of carrots and sticks gives you power, but it's hard to use these tools skillfully. Carrots lose their reward power when they're too abundant. Sticks lose their motivating power when they're overused. Many people have made carrots and sticks taboo, but without these natural tools, they find it hard to motivate themselves. They leave themselves prey to the carrots and sticks designed by others. You can learn to use carrots and sticks skillfully instead.

I am not suggesting that you actually use a stick on yourself, or your loved ones or coworkers. The point is that pain was the motivator of human history. The pain of hunger continued until you foraged successfully. Agriculture brought the risk of starving next year unless you take steps now. And if you didn't feel like milking the cow, you went without butter. Maybe your children went without milk.

Children grew up with an awareness of such threats in the past. They milked the cow and appreciated the butter. Today, children are freed from labor in order to study, but they get butter even if they refuse to study. They even critique the butter they get without an investment of effort. This wires them with unrealistic expectations about life.

Each brain has some glitches in its guidance system. These glitches can lead you astray when you need to tap into internal motivation. Fortunately, you can rewire your expectations about rewards and pain over time once you learn to notice them. You may deny that you care about a particular reward or pain with your verbal brain, but if a pathway is there, it is motivating you. If you have denied a pathway for a long time, it's scary to look straight at it. But an honest look at your myelinated GPS frees you to seek rewards and escape pain in new ways.

Let's start with the sticky subject of sticks since we have already explored the subject of rewards. Pain is nature's prime mover. Imagine a horse that refuses to budge no matter how many carrots you give it. You don't want to hit it with a stick, so you're completely stuck. There is nothing you can do but wait until the horse gets hungry. If you leave it for a few hours, carrots will become motivating again. If you think that is "abusive," then you are well and truly stuck.

When I was young, children were punished harshly by parents and teachers. Physical pain and rageful threats were common. Harsh management in the workplace was not unusual either. People learned to do what it takes to prevent pain, and learned some skills in the process. My generation objected to such practices, which is a great accomplishment. But we failed to replace them with an effective motivator. We presume another carrot will work, and when it doesn't, two carrots are offered. Then three.

The limits of this approach led to the "natural consequences" strategy. Children were supposed to learn from the consequences of their actions. They supposedly learn to be nice because no one will play with you if you are not nice. They are supposed to learn good work habits because your grades fall if you don't. But natural consequences often fail because the child brain is focused on the short run. Many schools undermine natural consequences by giving good grades to everyone and forcing children to include the aggressive playmate. Equality of rewards is mandated. Young brains learn from immediate rewards. Undesirable behaviors get wired in. As the verbal brain grows, it blames bad grades on the teacher, and blames social isolation on the other kids.

The failure of the natural consequences approach has led to a strategy of alarmism. We don't consciously call it "alarmism," but we resort to motivating young people with dire warnings. We tell them they will die if they choose the unwanted behavior. You will die if you drink and drive, or neglect to use a condom, or eat junk food. Children get used to hearing these urgent death threats. It becomes one of their core self-management tools. They fear they will die if they don't do everything right. Anxiety results.

How can we improve this arsenal of self-management tools?

Some people put a rubber band on their wrist to inflict pain when they engage in the unwanted behavior. But there are better ways to harness the natural motivating power of pain. Wasted time is a huge source of pain, and thus a useful tool. Time commitments are a great way to impose consequences on yourself. I discovered this when I resolved to bring plastic bags to the supermarket instead of wasting new bags. I kept forgetting the bags in my car. Each time, I'd resolve to remember them "next time," but next time never came. So I decided to inflict pain on myself by going back to the car whenever I forgot them. The first time I forgot, I said, "I'm too busy to go back today." I did that a few times, and then had a flash of insight. I was failing to keep a commitment to myself. I did not want to lose confidence in myself, so I went back to get those bags. And I didn't forget them again because I didn't want to waste the time. Well, the whole truth is that I forgot them again when I started shopping at a different store. The change in routine brought a new round of forgetting and I had to renew my commitment to myself and rebuild the habit.

It's hard to use sticks on yourself, but it's better than getting the stick from others. The better you can restrain yourself, the less you end up restrained by others.

Children hate external restraints. We hated being told when to go to bed. We thought life would be grand when we could decide that for ourselves. Today, you probably know the natural consequences of failing to get enough sleep. You are irritable and foggy the next day. But when you think of going to bed on time, you resist. That resistance is a myelinated pathway that opposes restraint, even when you're opposing yourself. Fortunately, you can build a new pathway with repetition. You can design the new path you need and repeat it until it gets established. You can design the carrots and sticks you need to motivate those steps. You can rewire yourself to feel pride (serotonin) when you live up to your commitments to yourself. You can learn to trust (oxytocin) in your new pathways, and feel excited (dopamine) by the new rewards you expect.

Jan's Story

Jan sees the enormity of the goal she has set for herself. She is trying to redirect her electricity from a huge highway to a tiny trail. She decides to help her inner mammal with a careful use of carrots and sticks.

The carrots are easy for Jan. She wants to invest some money into her photo projects. She decides to reward herself with one photo production every time she completes a week of daily practice of her taming tool. She really wants that reward, so she knows she will do it.

The stick is harder for her. She can't think of a stick that would work. Why beat herself for descending into anxiety in front of her daughter? More pain would only make things worse. But that urge to avoid pain reminds her that accountability has benefits. She creates accountability by breaking the challenge into small chunks. She resolves to delay her photo production by one day each time she spirals into her old wallowing and cringing habit. One day's delay of a photo order is not a huge punishment, but it's enough to keep her focused on her new intention. She wants those photo productions so much that she will keep redirecting her expectations.

Joe's Story

Joe is cooking! He thinks he has beaten that old habit of being the clean-up guy. He strives to focus on the positives of his contribution at work instead of on his negative reaction to others. He has done it for two weeks now, and his lasagna is widely celebrated by friends and family. Then it all starts to crash. First he overhears those jerks talking about him. They're saying everything he always feared. Then his boss asks to have a meeting with him. The boss's eyebrows were cocked at an ominous angle when he said it. The meeting is set for tomorrow. Joe goes home and eats cheesecake straight out of the freezer. He doesn't even notice until he's on the second slice. Then he can't think of what else to do, since he's sure the boss will submit to the jerks as always. He starts to defrost a slice of lasagna. It will taste bad after the cheesecake, of course. The disgusting thought of eating lasagna after cheesecake finally jolts his attention. What am I doing?

Joe is rewarding himself with food, of course. And he see that he needs a different reward in order to feel good about the challenge ahead of him. What would feel better than food? Telling the boss what he really thinks, of course! Telling all the jerks what he thinks. That sounds dangerous. Too dangerous. But Joe realizes that he can break it down into smaller steps. He can reveal his true thoughts in small doses to one person at a time. He can bring cheesecake to these meetings to ease the tension. They might hate him anyway, but he shouldn't give up without trying. He hates to admit that he has treated them like predators instead of explaining his perspective. He has made it easy for them to bond around a common enemy as mammals naturally do. It would not be very realistic of him to expect them to change after one conversation. He decides to express his true opinion once a day, and enjoy it. If he doesn't meet that goal, he commits to doing it twice the next day. And if he doesn't do that, he will take five minutes away from his cooking time to practice the joy of expressing himself in the privacy of his home.

REMEMBER:

1. Neglect of your needs feels like a threat, so listening to your needs makes you feel safe.

2. To spark serotonin, give yourself permission to take pride in something you've done. Take a step you're proud of each day and spend a minute appreciating yourself for it.

3. To spark oxytocin, create a moment of social trust by offering support and accepting the support offered to you. You can't always close the loop by making it reciprocal, but you can enjoy the trust you have.

4. To spark dopamine, find a new way to step toward an unmet need. Find a goal you can actually step toward rather than a dream that is always out of reach.

5. Distraction can be a valuable skill. It can shift your attention from threatening to unthreatening pathways to stop a cortisol spiral. You can't force yourself to be happy, but you can force yourself to focus on something other than potential threats.

6. Healthy distracters take time to cultivate, but they free you from distracters with harmful long-run consequences. The goal is not to be "good at it," but to be fully absorbed so your mind is not looking for threats.

7. Define your goals in a way that you have control over. You can always be stepping toward your goal if you have multiple goals and define them in terms of actions you can take.

8. Small steps go far if you keep taking them. Don't wait for others. They have their own path to find.

9. The mammal brain is motivated by rewards and pain, even if the verbal brain doesn't consciously think that.

10. Motivation is a problem when pain is taboo and rewards are so abundant that they've lost their motivating power. It takes conscious effort to design the carrots and sticks that work for you.

6

KEEPING IT
TAME IN THE LONG RUN

Our brain habituates to the rewards it has, so you can feel anxious
about losing something that didn't make you happy when you had it.

HABITUATION

What if you tame anxiety and it comes back?

This happens for a reason called "habituation" in biology. Our brain habituates to the rewards it has. It stops noticing them, so it takes something new to trigger happy chemicals. This is especially frustrating because you notice if you *lose* those rewards. Thus, you can feel anxious about losing something that didn't make you happy when you had it.

This impulse was demonstrated in monkeys by a landmark study at Cambridge University. Researchers trained monkeys to do a task in exchange for a spinach leaf. After a few days, the researchers suddenly switched to a bigger reward—a sip of juice. The monkeys' dopamine soared because sugar meets caloric needs more than spinach. The researchers continued to reward with juice, and after four days, the monkeys had no dopamine response. They literally took the juice for granted. The brain saves its dopamine for new information about rewards. Once you expect a reward, there's no new information and thus no dopamine. The monkeys' new expectations came from new dopamine pathways built in the first four days.

This study has an amazing twist because the researchers switched from juice back to spinach. The monkeys flew into a rage and threw the spinach back at the hand that fed them. They were provoked by the loss of a reward that didn't trigger their dopamine when they had it, and in fact were perfectly content with a week earlier. They now saw the world through the lens of new expectations, even thought they could not consciously articulate those expectations.

Humans experience the same paradox. We see the world through the lens of our dopamine past. When the world falls short of our expectations, we can surge with cortisol, even in the midst of a fine life. We're always eager for another dopamine surge because our brain evolved to seek it. Without it, we feel like something is missing.

Philosophers call this the "hedonic treadmill." You may feel like you are on a treadmill, never getting ahead and always at risk of falling behind. You have probably been taught to blame "our society" for the treadmill. That explanation leaves you feeling powerless and aggrieved, which is not good for you. You will start feeling powerful when you understand your own operating mammalian system.

The three-step taming tool can reap new rewards, but someday you may habituate to those rewards. The juice will stop exciting you, yet the risk of losing the juice fills you with fear. This chapter offers some tools for taming that paradox and finding new juice. Then it helps you master those tools throughout the life transitions that tend to magnify your ups and downs.

Habituation and Anxiety

If you were thirsty in the desert, the sight of a distant waterhole would fill you with joy. But in your life today, endless running water doesn't make you happy. It can even make you anxious as you ponder threats to your water. This conundrum is easier to manage when you remember the useful purpose of habituation. Our ancestors survived because their brains focused on unmet needs. In a world of scarcity, unmet needs are obvious and pressing. To understand that, imagine you're on a camping trip. At first, the novelty of the surroundings triggers your dopamine joy. But soon you are hungry, cold, and tired, so you focus on the next step toward relieving your most urgent discomfort. Each time you relieve a discomfort, you feel good. The more uncomfortable you are, the easier it is to find a way to feel better.

After the camping trip, your physical needs are more easily met. Now you have to find other needs to meet in order to feel good. That challenge is complicated by your myelinated pathways. They trigger expectations about good feelings, yet the good feelings somehow fail to come. If you don't understand myelination and habituation, you keep trying the same things, and failing to get the desired happiness. You decide that something is wrong with the world.

And to make life harder still, serotonin and oxytocin habituate too.

Habituation and Social Rewards

Your oxytocin surges when that special someone notices you, but if that person becomes a regular part of your life, the surge stops. Your brain stops seeing that person as new information. And with your needs met, you don't have that joy of meeting an unmet need. The point is not that you should have affairs. The point is that you should understand oxytocin. You can value the steady drip of oxytocin in your daily life instead of risking everything for one big spurt. And you can stimulate more oxytocin by building new trust bonds that are not based on romance.

It's the same with serotonin. You got a big spurt when you won the talent show, but soon the applause is over. The serotonin stops, even though you are still the person who won the talent show. You still get a drip when you think about it, but your brain evolved to crave another spurt. It expects to find it in ways that worked before, so you can end up investing a lot of energy in a quest for applause. It's easy to sneer when others do this, but it's useful to recognize your own longing for serotonin. Perhaps you stimulate it with a quest for a big promotion. Once you get the big promotion, your brain habituates, and it takes a new source of social recognition to stimulate it. But losing the great job is always possible, and your cortisol flows when you think about that. So you end up suffering over a job that doesn't make you happy.

Even if you discovered a new planet, your inner mammal would be on this treadmill. At first, you'd be thrilled each morning when you remembered your planet, but in a short time, the thrill would mysteriously disappear. Your brain would look for ways to get it back, and it would seem like you need to discover another planet. You start seeing up-and-coming astronomers as survival threats, despite your good intentions.

To complicate life further, we often have to sacrifice one happy chemical to get more of another. Spending time at the office may get you the serotonin-boosting promotion but cost you oxytocin at home. When you stay home, however, you miss the serotonin you got at work. Or you may have the opposite wiring: you get oxytocin at work from a sense of belonging with coworkers, and you get serotonin at home where you're treated like you're special. However you're wired, uncomfortable trade-offs are part of life. Your promotion may cost you the acceptance of your coworkers, so your oxytocin goes down as your serotonin goes up. You can grieve the loss of oxytocin, or you can enjoy the serotonin and design new oxytocin steps. It's your choice.

You can say we shouldn't have to choose. You can say everyone should applaud everyone else all the time. But it's just not realistic. Your coworkers are mammals. Your loved ones are mammals. You are a mammal too.

A gazelle constantly faces uncomfortable trade-offs between the herd and greener pastures. When you face uncomfortable trade-offs, it helps to know that your brain is designed to make those choices. All mammals do it.

Habituation and Addiction

The first time you ate a brownie, it was the best brownie you ever had. That surge of joy built a pathway that motivates you to seek brownies, but if you eat another brownie tomorrow, it is no longer the best you've ever had. You miss that "best-ever" feeling and look for a way to get it back.

Addiction is widely seen as a quest for that first high. It's hard to get that with a brain that habituates to good things. But you still expect it, because your brain got wired by past experience. So if one brownie doesn't trigger it, you may think a second brownie is needed.

Extra-large reward circuits trigger extra-large motivation. For example, the rewards you experienced in adolescence were easily myelinated, making it easy to keep expecting a reward even if it keeps disappointing you. Another example is any reward you experienced in a moment of threat. Your brain prioritizes anything that relieves threats. So whatever relieved your threatened feelings in adolescence built your biggest reward pathways. In time, habituation limits the reward feeling, but the pathways remain.

You also build an extra-large reward circuit if you expose yourself to an unnatural reward, because it is more rewarding than anything you can get naturally. For example, cocaine gives you a bigger jolt of dopamine than you could get from daily life. Heroin supplies more endorphin than you get from daily life. Pornography triggers more chemistry than real life. But your brain habituates to even the extra-large input of artificial rewards, which motivates you to seek even more. It's hard to get excited about natural rewards as a result. Extra-large neural pathways make it feel like the artificial reward is good for your survival, even when it obviously is not.

Our brain is designed to look for the best return on its efforts. Addiction is a pathway that promises a big reward for your efforts. The promise is disappointed, but the circuit remains, motivating more focus on that reward. The solution is to build new pathways to expect new rewards. This is not easy when the old pathway got a boost from artificial rewards, adolescence, and the relief of pain. But with repetition, a new pathway will build.

Some people say intoxication is natural because monkeys imbibe when they have the chance. This is false, and it's easy to see why with a close look at alcohol in nature. Fruit produces alcohol when it's past its prime. Animals dislike the taste and avoid the fruit, so alcohol protects animals from eating rotten fruit. But when food is scarce, hunger will drive an animal to eat it anyway. The animal gets too tipsy to keep eating, which again limits consumption of rotten fruit. Animals do not try to get tipsy, and they would not survive for long if they did. Alcohol-seeking animals would quickly be weeded out of the gene pool.

So why are we told that animals seek alcohol? One reason is that monkeys steal mai tais from vacationers at tropical resorts. Many monkeys have been caught chugging on video. But monkeys did not evolve in a world of resort mai tais. They evolved in a world where sugar was a huge reward because calories were hard to come by. A monkey would have to spend a lot of time chewing green leaves to get the energy in a cocktail, so its brain sees the cocktail as a big reward.

The myth of party animals was reinforced by rat studies purporting to show that rats prefer alcohol to water. Of course the rat's brain is good at detecting the sugar in the alcohol. Pampered lab rats never have to deal with the consequences of intoxication. This creates the illusion that intoxication is desirable in nature when the reality is quite the opposite.

When the Party's Over

What happens when the thing you love stops feeling good?
It feels like a blast of cortisol.
Even when you're perfectly safe, you feel threatened when a good feeling ends because happy chemicals mask the stresses of daily life. When the mask falls and those stresses return to your awareness, it's easy to believe you are actually threatened. And it's easy to rush for more of your familiar reward, even though its effect is disappointing. For example, imagine a gambler who longs for the familiar thrill. One day at the casino, the gambler isn't feeling the thrill, so they rush into bigger stakes. The more they

seek feelings that mask reality, the worse their reality gets, and the more motivated they are to mask it.

We all long for the thrill of happy chemicals because they mask cortisol. The more safe ways you know to seek them, the more you protect yourself from harmful ways to seek them. But in that moment when your old thrill is gone, alternatives may not sound appealing. Cortisol motivates you to do something fast. What can you do?

Sit with the bad feeling for one minute. This valuable skill teaches your brain that the bad feeling doesn't actually kill you. Each time you face the dragon, you build the circuit that trusts your power against the dragon. Each time you run from the dragon, you build the circuit that fears the dragon. Stop running and the dragon will start to seem tamer.

Our happy chemicals are not designed to surge all the time. They are designed to droop after they surge, and we are designed to live with the droop. A monkey's dopamine droops after it finally gets the mango it was climbing toward. Without that excitement, the monkey is more aware of other things going on around it. But it will not manufacture threats, because its cortex isn't big enough. It will not rush for another mango to mask the bad feeling of a manufactured threat. It will rest and digest for a moment and then choose a step toward an unmet need. You can call it their neutral gear.

When your happy chemicals droop, it helps to think of this as your neutral gear. It protects you from overreacting to the sudden inrush of reality after pleasure subsides. Neutral is natural, not a crisis. Neutral frees you to define your next need and your next step.

If you were a pioneer on the Oregon Trail, finding berries would have thrilled you with dopamine. If you were told about the berries from the start, you would have anticipated the excitement through weeks of trudging through harsh terrain. If a time-travel machine brought that pioneer to a modern supermarket, they'd be ecstatic. Yet supermarkets don't thrill us today because the reward is already expected.

HOPE AT LAST

When old rewards lose their thrill, how can you replace them in healthy ways?

An interesting solution is presented in Csikszentmihalyi's book, *Flow*. He uses the example of a piece of music that lifts your mood when you're down. If you listened to that music all the time, it would eventually lose that effect. Now how can you lift your mood?

Music stimulates dopamine because your brain is constantly anticipating the next sound and feeling rewarded when it finds an input that fits what it anticipated. Each match stimulates a drip of dopamine, and then you move on to the next match and the next dopamine drip. Music that is too familiar doesn't trigger much dopamine because sound flows effortlessly into an old pathway without the seek-and-find effort. Music that is too unfamiliar doesn't trigger much dopamine because you can't make successful predictions. The sweet spot between familiar and unfamiliar makes music feel good. Now you have a dilemma because the music you enjoy will eventually become too familiar. So if you want to feel good, invest some time in unfamiliar music to the point where it becomes predictable, but not too predictable. Start now so you will have that pleasure by the time an old pleasure wears out. You may not be in the mood for this today since you still enjoy your old favorites. And you may not be in the mood for it when your pleasure is gone and anxiety makes it hard to focus on the unfamiliar. That's why this effective tool often goes unused.

This tool works for much more than music. Many of life's pleasures work the same way. For example, a sport may not be fun the first time you play, and a craft may be frustrating the first time you try it. Great pleasure can be found in skills and social rituals that do not feel good at first. That's because our cortex is a pattern-matching engine. Experience wires in patterns, and when you find a new input that matches a stored pattern, dopamine is your reward. Bigger patterns bring bigger dopamine rewards.

You can stay in the sweet spot if you keep wiring in new patterns. This strategy can enhance rewards in all areas of life. Start building new career skills before you hate your job. Start cooking new foods before boredom leads you to overeat. Start building new social bonds before you get bitter about the old bonds.

I am not saying you should queue up new lovers to be ready when an old romance fades. It bears repeating that long-term relationships have advantages. You have someone who knows who you are when you barely remember yourself. Long-term relationships are easier to sustain when you manage your own droop instead of blaming it on the other person.

You can cultivate new pleasures instead of limiting yourself to primal pleasures. You can manage the "been-there/done-that" feeling instead of blaming it on your friends, your boss, or your leaders.

LIFE CYCLE ANXIETY

Anxiety is often blamed on the stage of life one is in, from childhood insecurities to teen angst, to college stress, career transition, parenting woes, empty nest syndrome, retirement, and aging. A whole life of anxiety can result if you take this view. Instead, you can tame anxiety by looking at the life cycle from the mammal brain's perspective.

Existential Angst

Death is an abstraction, so animals don't think about it. When you attach a human cortex to a mammalian limbic system, you get a brain that can terrorize itself with awareness of its own mortality. Our brain urgently strives for survival with the knowledge that it will fail someday. We don't know what will kill us, so we never know if we are safe.

The brain tries to ease this terror by creating something that will survive. Procreation was nature's way of doing that. Animals aren't consciously promoting the survival of their genes, but their brain makes them feel good when they do that. We have inherited a brain that makes us feel good when we promote the survival of our unique individual essence. Before the age of birth control, children were your primary legacy, because you had little energy left for other things after you provided for them. If you were lucky enough to reach middle age, you saw grandchildren carrying on your traditions. That stimulates the good feeling of survival, which eases existential angst. And if you had more energy, you created more things that would survive, whether hand-made tools or granite temples.

In the age of birth control, we can make decisions about where to invest our energy. But today, for one reason or another, few people have the comfort of watching grandchildren carry on their traditions. Thus, we are more eager to create other things that survive. Whether it's a work of art, an institution, children, or your legendary chili recipe, creating something immortal helps ease mortal fears. Throughout human history, people have made colossal sacrifices to build a legacy.

But it's complicated, because every threat to your creation now feels like a survival threat. Any criticism of your art, your grandchildren, or your chili triggers life-or-death feelings. And you believe it's a real threat because you don't understand your natural urge to leave a legacy.

Death had a big presence for most of human history because more people died younger and at home. Today we strive to avoid the inevitable.

We direct our anxiety at the health care system without acknowledging the existential fear that drives it. The more energy you direct into your legacy, the less you waste on anxiety.

The legacy urge has tremendous motivating power, but we often overlook it because it's nonverbal. Animals can help us understand the power of the urge to promote one's unique individual essence. Male chimpanzees are only interested in females that are actively fertile. This only happens once in five years because lactation for each newborn continues for four years. Male chimps invest five years struggling with other males in order to be in a position of strength at the right moment. Conscious knowledge of biology is not required, because the mammal brain rewards behaviors that build its legacy. (Female chimps are equally motivated to promote their legacy; they jockey with other females for resources that promote the survival of their young.)

You may not use the word "legacy." You may think it sounds pretentious. But your anxiety abates when you promote the survival of your unique essence. "Changing the world" stimulates that legacy feeling, which makes it very alluring. But it's a two-edged sword, because every obstacle to your desired change now feels like a survival threat.

It helps to look directly at the link between legacy and happy chemicals. Serotonin is triggered by the social importance your contribution is expected to bring. Oxytocin is triggered by the sense of belonging your legacy gives you. Dopamine is triggered by the anticipation of serotonin and oxytocin. You don't need to be a tribal chieftain or a celebrity superstar to enjoy this feeling. Your brain scans for whatever legacy options you can find because it feels good.

No matter what choices you make, someday there will be a future that you will not be part of. The world will spin on without you. This thought is so distressing that cortisol is often triggered by thoughts of the future. You hear talk about decline and collapse in fiction and nonfiction, and it feels true because it fits the pattern you have already activated. Thoughts of cosmic decline divert you from more distressing thoughts of your own decline. But declinism is a big source of anxiety. You can relieve this anxiety by focusing on your own legacy.

The Empty Space

When you lose something that met your needs, threatened feelings grow. If it's a sad loss, like a death or divorce, the bad feeling makes sense, but we often feel threatened by happy losses, like graduating, retiring, or watching your child become independent. An empty space leaves you without your usual way of masking cortisol.

If you were fighting cancer, you'd feel great when you won. But then you would have an empty space, because your needs would no longer be defined by the fight against cancer. This feels surprisingly bad. The same is true if you're escaping a war zone or training for a marathon or searching for a life partner. You think you will be happy forever when you reach that goal, but now that you're there, your next step toward good feelings is hard to define.

For much of life, your next step seems so urgent that you don't have to think about it. You rush to prepare for the next exam or put the next meal on the table or put out the next fire. When the rush is over, it's hard to choose your next step because you are not in the habit of choosing. And without a next step to focus on, cortisol gets your attention. You may see the cortisol as a real crisis and rush to mask it in unhealthy ways. But when you know how your brain works, you realize that your distress is caused by an empty space. You can use the three-step taming tool to rebuild your sense of direction.

The Fall from Grace

Sometimes life hands you a big drop in status. You can say you don't care about status, but it feels surprisingly bad.

Sometimes your fall from grace has an obvious cause, like lost love or a financial setback. But sometimes the cause is so subtle that you don't consciously notice. Perhaps you did something you know is wrong and lost your sense of moral superiority. Or you compare yourself to someone who has just had a big jump in status. What matters is your own perception, not the labels used by others. When you feel like you've taken a fall, your serotonin takes a beating.

The mammal brain cares about status because that promotes survival in the state of nature. Higher-ranking monkeys have more surviving offspring, and natural selection has built a brain that has life-or-death feelings about its status. This is why a fall from grace can drench you in cortisol, even when your life is better than the wildest imaginings of your ancestors.

To escape this distress, create a frame of reference that puts you in the one-up position. You may think this is crude or delusional, but you have already created a frame of reference that puts you in the one-down position. That is depriving you of serotonin. Your grief is caused by an abstraction, so you need to replace it with a healthier abstraction. For most of human history, getting revenge was the automatic way of restoring one-upness. It has taken millennia to stop the revenge cycles that resulted. Today, we look for healthy, nonviolent ways to raise our status. You can say we shouldn't compare ourselves to others, but the mammal brain keeps going there. So choose a path you can be proud of and start taking steps. (More on this in chapter 8 on pitfalls.)

The Perfect Storm

Multiple setbacks can assault you at the same time. Your power is hard to feel when it's drained in many directions. Fortunately, it only takes one step toward rewards to spark chemicals that ease the next step. You can find this step if you take a full minute to define your needs, twenty minutes to metabolize your cortisol, and a minute to define a step to take right now. Small drips of good feelings build a circuit that expects more good feelings. You build trust in your ability to meet your needs, which is what makes a mammal feel safe.

It's harder to do this if you are surrounded by an anxiety mind-set. The people who are "helping" you may support your anxiety instead of supporting your steps to relieve it. In the short run, this kind of "help" can reward you with the oxytocin of social trust. It can also give you serotonin if it puts you in the one-up position. And it brings dopamine if this is the only reward path you know. In the long run, alas, the anxiety mind-set means endless pain. You are better off with the three-step tool than with help that doesn't help. (More on this in chapter 10 on help.)

REMEMBER:

1. Our brain habituates to the rewards it has. It stops noticing them, so it takes something new to trigger happy chemicals.
2. Losing a habitual reward triggers cortisol, so you can feel anxious about losing something that didn't make you happy when you had it.
3. When your physical needs are met, your brain looks to social rewards. But the brain habituates to social rewards as it does for physical rewards.
4. Steps toward one happy-chemical reward may undermine your prospects for another reward. Our brain evolved to manage these uncomfortable trade-offs.

5. Habituation means you don't actually get the good feelings you expect from rewards you have enjoyed before. But you are still motivated to seek those rewards because the pathway is still there.

6. Addiction is the expectation of big rewards built from past experience of big rewards. Habituation diminishes the reward, but you keep expecting it because the big experience built a big circuit. The solution is to build new reward circuits by experiencing new rewards repeatedly.

7. Alcohol is produced naturally by rotting fruit. It helps protect animals from the threat of eating rotten fruit.

8. If you sit with a bad feeling for one minute, you teach your brain that the bad feeling doesn't kill you.

9. Our happy chemicals are not designed to surge all the time. They are designed to droop after they surge. This neutral state is when a mammal chooses the next unmet need to step toward.

10. The pleasure of dopamine lies in the sweet spot between too familiar and too unfamiliar. All pleasures become more familiar over time. To replace them, we must invest effort in something unfamiliar until it reaches the sweet spot.

11. The human brain is aware of its own mortality. Creating something that survives helps to ease our existential angst. But we pay a high price for this comfort, because every threat to your legacy now feels like a survival threat.

12. Your happy chemicals are especially responsive to activities that promote the survival of your unique individual essence.

13. An empty space allows anxiety to get your attention, whether the empty space is caused by a happy loss or an unhappy loss.

14. A loss of status triggers threatened feelings in the mammal brain. Thoughts that raise your status will relieve these threatened feelings.

15. It only takes one step toward rewards to spark chemicals that ease the next step.

7

STOCK YOUR PANTRY
WITH ANXIETY TAMERS

*The world cannot provide the complete sense of security that we long
for at birth. You have to knit that sense together for yourself.*

You have probably learned to stock your home with healthy food so
you don't yield to junk food in a moment of weakness. You can
do the same with non-food rewards. Stock your life with healthy anxiety
tamers and you will be less tempted by harmful junk. (Food is discussed
separately in the following chapter.)

A healthy reward is something that feels good in the short run and
doesn't have bad consequences in the long run. You may think healthy
rewards are scarce! That's because they are only rewarding if you build
circuits to appreciate them. Unhealthy rewards feel good effortlessly, by
contrast, because our brain evolved to respond to them.

Pleasure is the brain's signal that you are meeting a need. A person
who takes pleasure in bird-watching does not meet a primal survival need
by indulging in that activity, but something in that person's past has connected bird-watching to primal needs. Bird-watching can stimulate oxytocin if it connects you to others. It can stimulate serotonin when you enjoy
a sense of accomplishment. It stimulates dopamine when you scan for an
expected pattern and then find it. And it can relieve cortisol by distracting
you from perceived threats. Yet most people do not enjoy bird-watching.
I don't either.

Each brain defines rewards with circuits built from experience. It's
easy to wire yourself for unhealthy rewards because nature gives you a head
start. But you can build new circuits to enjoy new rewards. You can find
pleasure without harmful long-run consequences. This chapter introduces
a universe of possibilities.

This chapter is not about exercise and nutrition, although these rewards are popular strategies for relieving anxiety. If they work for you, great. But many people do not find them rewarding. This chapter will help you find rewards you actually enjoy so you can turn to them in a moment of distress. You still need exercise and nutrition for your physical health, but you need pleasure for your mental health. Diet and exercise should be on your to-do list, but an endless to-do list does not relieve anxiety. So alongside your list of things that are good for you, you need a list of things that are fun for you.

1. WORK YOUR BODY AND MIND TOGETHER

An activity that works mind and body together is a very effective way to redirect your energy. Many popular pastimes do this, such as crafts, cooking, playing a musical instrument, playing with a pet, art, sports, and gardening. When you synchronize mind and body, you activate so many circuits that you can't dwell on threats. You literally forget to worry.

In the past, mind–body activities were essential to survival. You baked bread because there was no other way to get bread. You planted beans in order to eat beans. Today you can meet your basic needs with less physical activity, but your brain needs this activity to feel good. Many people focus on physical activity that's not fun, like optimizing your heart rate at the gym. You can find a way to add fun to your physical activity. It may not be aerobic but it drains your stress circuits.

What's fun for you depends on the circuits you have and the effort you are willing to invest in circuit-building. A good place to start is an activity you always wished you had time for. But once you make time for it, monitor your state of mind. Can you do it without getting too frustrated? Can you do it without dwelling on anxieties? Some people love a walk in the park, but other people spend the whole time stewing over past annoyances, or finding fault with things they see in the park. If you do that, find a different activity.

Keep experimenting until you find an activity that fully engages your mind. Can you bake a cake without replaying family dramas in your mind? Can you play pool without dwelling on work tensions? Can you do yoga without critiquing the world and yourself while you're holding a pose? The more complex the activity, the better it absorbs you. Complex activities spark more circuits, but those circuits take time to build.

My favorite taming tool is to watch something in a foreign language while stretching. I understand Romance languages if I read the English at the same time, but it takes so much focus that I completely forget whatever was on my mind. Instead of sitting still while I watch, I stand and twist, kick, bend, jump, and flail for twenty minutes. A physical therapist recommended this movement strategy, and I thought it was stupid at first. Now, it's a very welcome diversion from my day at the keyboard.

Be sure to have a mind-body activity you can do away from home as well. My favorite is listening to a comedy recording while walking up and down stairs. When I go to a stressful meeting, I know I can always head for the staircase, prepared with a recording that drains my electricity away from anxious thoughts.

When your brain is half busy, stressful thoughts can easily drift in. When you listen to music, for example, one thought can lead to another and you can find yourself spiraling before you realize it. If this happens to you, add movement to your listening. If it happens while you lift weights, listen to something uplifting while you lift.

Keeping it fun is essential. You have the rest of your life to work on your abs or impress the world with your art. You need to give yourself twenty minutes to excrete cortisol by engaging in something you like. Whether you tend cactus plants or crochet socks, what matters is that you like it. Then you will have a positive feeling as you move into your next step. And you'll do it without calories, legal trouble, or impairing your ability to operate heavy machinery.

2. MIRROR A TAME PERSON

Our brains have special neurons designed to mirror others. These *mirror neurons* only activate when you see another individual get rewards or suffer pain. They trigger the same pattern you would experience if you got the reward or suffered the pain yourself, though with less intensity. This activation makes it easier for you to initiate the steps needed to get that reward or avoid that harm yourself.

It's easy to see how this works with monkeys. In the monkey world, eating a nut is a huge reward because it's a huge nutritional boost. They don't know that, but the fat and protein trigger a huge dopamine surge. Cracking open a nut is very hard for monkeys, alas. And no one cracks them for you, even your mother. So a monkey has to build cracking skills before it can get the nutrition necessary for strong muscles. Monkeys learn to crack nuts by mirroring others. Sometimes it takes them years to learn the skill. Each time they fail, they stare at others that succeed. They literally get the feel of it without need for words.

You have been mirroring people all your life. You see people get rewards and avoid harm, and it activates your brain. The behaviors you mirrored repeatedly in youth built big pathways. Some of those pathways are helpful today, and some need a bit of redirection. You can help yourself do that by choosing new people to mirror. Find a tame person and observe. You will spark a circuit for a tame response.

For example, I had a bad reaction when my dentist told me to floss. I couldn't imagine doing such a difficult thing late at night. Then I married my husband and saw him floss. He acted like it was effortless. I couldn't believe that was possible until I saw it myself. Suddenly, I felt like I could do it too. I didn't do it exactly his way. I created a routine that met my own needs. I made it fun by doing it at 9 p.m. in front of the television with fla-vored floss. Soon it became a habit and my dentist sees a big improvement.

You will not find a perfect person to mirror because we are all bundles of strengths and weaknesses. You can mirror one trait in one person and another trait in another person. As you shop for behaviors to mirror, keep an eye out for people who are good at defining their needs, engaging in de-stressing activities, and taking action steps. If they can do it, you can do it.

Mirror neurons work without cognition. Your verbal brain doesn't "know" how the other person does it, but somehow you "know." A baby monkey doesn't "know" that it needs nuts. It just sees others get eager about an object in their hand, so it picks the crumbs left in their shells. That triggers dopamine, which enhances the expectation of reward. So they watch and try and watch and try until they get it.

We have all been exposed to some undesirable behaviors in youth. You told yourself "I will never do that," but sometimes you are shocked to find yourself doing it. A child has limited control over the people available to mirror. Now you have a choice. When you understand mirror neurons, you make careful decisions about whose behavior you expose yourself to. Don't surround yourself with raging anger or quiet despair. Find yourself some calm confidence to mirror. It may not be everywhere, but you can find moments and build a circuit.

Mirroring can aggravate your social-comparison impulse if you let it. You may feel like everyone else is getting nuts and you are left out. You may end up with a cortisol surge that only detracts from your nut-cracking skills. Fortunately, mirroring can improve your cortisol-management skills as well as your reward-seeking skills. The following chapter will address the social comparison pitfall in more detail.

3. VARIETY

We have seen that habituation erodes pleasure. Variety is the best way to restore it. For example, if you drink coffee every morning, you take it for granted and hardly notice. You long for a second cup, and maybe a third. If you only had coffee every other day, you would really notice it when you had it. This is a way to enjoy coffee without overdoing it. On the no-coffee days, you can find an alternative pleasure. It takes some effort to wire in alternative healthy pleasures, but the reward is worth the effort.

This strategy can work with alcohol or snack foods as well. Limiting yourself to one drink or one cookie on alternate days can help you control that urge for more. Variety can also enhance the pleasure of your entertainment or athletic activities. Explore new pleasures before the old ones feel dull. Sample new sports, books, entertainment, hobbies, or foods to give your brain variety. Dig the well before you need the water! (It bears repeating that I am not advocating intimacy with strangers, since that has well-known drawbacks.)

Variety can also expand the pleasure of social trust. If you rely on the same people all the time, you may eventually feel disappointed. No one can understand you on every issue and agree with you on every choice. If you expect that, you will just end up resentful and undermine whatever rapport you have. Instead, you can seek understanding from a variety of people. You can find one person who understands you in one aspect of life, and others who understand you in other aspects. You will weave a mature feeling of being understood instead of wallowing in a childlike sense of abandonment. The world cannot provide the complete sense of security that we long for at birth. You have to knit that sense together for yourself.

Of course it's hard to try something new in a moment of distress, so it's useful to start your exploring when you're feeling good. I do my exploring around dinner time, when my productivity is off-peak but I still have some focus. The time you invest in discovering new rewards will pay big dividends in the future. Variety replenishes your anxiety-taming toolbox so you can always meet your needs.

4. LAUGH

Laughing is the sustainable way to get endorphin into your life. Real laughs are what trigger it because they activate *intrinsic muscles* that are sometimes ignored. You can have more laughter if you make it a priority. This is hard, you may say. The world may not seem very funny. You're busy. You can't force it. But there are some things you can do to get more laughs in your life.

Redefine Laughter

You may be restraining your laughs for one reason or another. Maybe you think they look silly. If you start to see laughter as a strength, rather than a weakness, your laughs will be released.

Laughter is a sudden relief of perceived threat. Physical comedy is relief from a physical threat and verbal comedy is relief from threats perceived by the verbal brain. Comedy reinterprets a potential threat so it's safe to lower your guard. Laughter is the sudden relief of muscle tension that a lowered guard allows. You may think lowering your guard is dangerous due to real past experience. The endorphin of laughter can retrain your brain to feel safe when your guard is down.

Make Time for Comedy

If you say you have no time for comedy, it's like saying you're too full to eat vegetables. You need to make room.

You may think most comedy is "not funny." I agree. Each of us has to shop for the comedy that appeals to us. That takes time, so you need to make time in order to have something funny in your pantry when you need it. In a busy world, it seems strange to devote time to shopping for comedy. But the expression, "There's never enough time to do it right, but there's always enough time to do it over," reminds us that "There's never enough time to laugh, but there's always enough time for anxiety." In the long run, laughter makes time for itself.

Prioritize Your Own Sense of Humor

Humor that appeals to your friends and family may not appeal to you. If you concede to their taste all the time, you deprive yourself of laughter. You need to make space for your own sense of humor regardless of who else it appeals to.

I dislike the angry, bitter kind of humor, but I found an improv theater that always cracks me up. I was eager to bring everyone I know to this theater and was surprised when my guests didn't like it. Sometimes their displeasure ruined my fun, so now I just go with my husband. We appreciate having something we love instead of worrying about other people's taste.

5. THE RUBBER DUCKY METHOD

I was surprised to learn that software engineers relieve threats with "the rubber ducky method." When a coder confronts a tough debugging problem, they are advised to explain the problem to a rubber ducky. Literally. A solution often emerges in a few minutes.

I loved hearing this because it gave me a word for something I already did. My husband is my rubber ducky. I vent to him when I can't get an app to work, and the answer usually comes to me while I'm speaking. Then I'm embarrassed to have bothered him, so I explain that I was absolutely stuck before I called him. My husband doesn't know the apps I work with, so he usually can't help anyway. But when he hears a scream from my office, he kindly offers to help. Now that I understand my brain, I just say, "Can I please explain my problem to you because it often helps." It's hard to believe that it works, since I truly feel like I've tried everything before I call him. But it works so well that now he uses me as his rubber ducky.

This method helped me solve a bigger emotional problem. I used to feel sad about not having a herd. For most of my life, I thought others had "a great support system," and I somehow missed out. I know this is an old pattern from my childhood. My mother felt bad about her lack of support and modeled this for me. I also know that everyone longs for more support because we're all born vulnerable. And I know that people who sell "support" are marketing the belief that others have a cozy support system. But for all my insight, my inner mammal felt like something was missing. Then I heard about the rubber ducky method and started thinking more realistically. If you can get support from a piece of yellow plastic, then support is just a feeling you create in your own neurons.

The support of a rubber ducky is the best kind of support in certain ways. Human beings might easily be offended if you don't take their advice. And I might be offended by their failure to understand my problem. A rubber ducky doesn't create these problems. It makes me grateful for my freedom to choose my own solutions instead of being pressured into solutions I dislike. It's hard to trust my own wisdom when I'm stuck, but talking to a rubber ducky helps my inner mammal and my verbal brain trust each other. Then they can work together on a solution.

Of course I would love to have someone who knows the right answer about everything. But that is the longing of a child. In adulthood, my problems are too specific for another person to see from my perspective, just as I cannot see other people's problems from their perspective. If I depended on someone to solve my problems, I would end up stepping toward what that person wants rather than what I want. So I am glad I have the chance to call my own shots. Instead of wasting energy on a quest for the perfect adviser, I invest my energy gathering different opinions and connecting the dots for myself.

The rubber ducky method helped me understand why so many people long for support and then resent the support they get. When you have a problem, you are embedded in the details of that problem. No one can understand it the way you do. Getting upset about that is futile. You might just as well get angry at a duck-shaped piece of plastic.

6. SELF-EXPRESSION

An infant must express itself to get its needs met. Relief comes when it makes a noise, which wires the newborn brain to expect relief when it makes a noise. A child soon makes more complex sounds in its quest to get relief from others. Self-expression is our core tool for feeling safe.

Maturity increases your ability to meet your own needs, but your brain still expects to get relief by communicating your needs to others. Sometimes you get the support you seek and sometimes you don't, yet you still connect self-expression to relief because the circuits are so well developed.

Humans have always sought comfort in self-expression, though our ways of doing it change with time. Prayer was a popular strategy for most of human history. Writing letters or poetry was popular in centuries past. Social media is popular today. We are influenced by the self-expression strategies of those around us.

You may romanticize the self-expression of the past. Heart-warming images of people telling stories around the campfire are widely conveyed. We imagine these people having perfect mutual understanding, but if you lived in that world, you would be bored with hearing the same stories since you were born, and you would be frustrated when other people's stories got more attention than yours.

The same is true for letter-writing and poetry. These pre-electronic social media are idealized today, but the people who wrote them were like us. They appealed for the support of others and got ignored sometimes, despite their great eloquence. They felt obligated by the long-winded appeals for support from others. If you like low-tech forms of self-expression, no one is stopping you from writing poems and telling stories around a campfire. Maybe it seems like no one will listen and you blame that on technology. But if you were born before technology, your message would be competing with everyone else's in whatever media were available.

The real problem is the urge to be heard in a world where everyone else has the urge to be heard. And that is only a problem if you make it one. Instead, you can accept your natural urge for attention. Sometimes your self-expression will be drowned out by the expressions of others, and this will feel like a threat. When you know the cause of this threatened feeling, you have power over it. When you deny your natural urge for attention, you don't know where the threatened feeling is coming from, so you think it's a real threat.

People have always competed for attention, with whatever technology emerged when they emerged. People have always struggled to be heard because it stimulates serotonin or oxytocin. These good feelings are soon metabolized, so people are always seeking more. If you don't get it, your happy chemicals droop. This droop is not a crisis; it's the motivational mechanism built by natural selection.

As we grow in experience, we learn to modify our message to improve our chances of getting heard. There are always difficult trade-offs between the expression that comes to you naturally and the expression you expect to get results. With maturity, you can make these trade-offs consciously.

There is no perfect choice between authenticity and results. Doing the popular thing may get results, but you end up feeling stifled. Authentic self-expression brings more relief but may fail to be heard. You want both, so you constantly adjust your message in hopes of getting the pleasure of authenticity and the pleasure of recognition at the same time. But you fail. When you get recognition, you feel a stifling pressure to conform to expectations. When you focus on your own mind-set and ignore the mind-set of others, you feel a scary disconnection. Your brain focuses on the unmet need, so it always feels like something is wrong. You can retrain yourself to focus on what is right instead of what is wrong. You can enjoy recognition when it happens and enjoy authenticity when that happens. You can enjoy the act of expressing yourself regardless of the immediate response.

Children are often rewarded for modes of expression that undermine their rewards in adulthood. Some children get rewarded when they scream, and other children get rewarded when they censor themselves. Both of these patterns have drawbacks in adulthood. It's foolish to think others got the perfect training and you got shortchanged. There is no perfect self-expression strategy. We all scream at times and censor ourselves at other times. We all keep fine-tuning our self-expression. Old pathways can limit that, so it's great to find your power to build new pathways.

Our ancestors found comfort in self-expression even when their direst appeals went unanswered. They appealed to rain gods when drought threatened their survival, and consulted shamans to target their message more effectively. It's easy to sneer at these strategies today, but most of us have not lived with the threat of starvation or annihilation. Instead of enjoying our good fortune, we equate small disappointments with annihilation. Anxiety is the result. We can relieve it by learning from the rituals of darker days. Our ancestors prayed to rain gods but they also developed irrigation and food storage methods to meet their needs. We are safe from hunger today because our ancestors expressed their needs and then took steps to meet them.

The animal perspective helps to clarify our drive for self-expression. As noted in chapter 3, when you hear animals calling out, most of the time they are saying, "I'm here, where are you?" and waiting for a reply of "I'm here, where are you?" This is what makes a mammal feel safe. If you did that, people would think you were annoying. Instead, you have to work hard to get the world to respond in the way your inner mammal longs for. When you don't get it, your mammal brain releases survival-threat feelings. It's hard to make sense of these feelings because your verbal brain won't admit that it cares. When you understand this chemical sense of urgency, you can enjoy self-expression despite the inevitable risk.

7. REWARD YOURSELF WITH FREE TIME

Free time may be the reward you want more than anything else, and you have the power to get it. But you may be absolutely convinced that you can't have it because you are too busy for a break. People who refuse to have downtime often resort to unhealthy ways of taking a break. You reward yourself with something bad for your body or bad for your mind when you would have been happier to just have some free time.

Smoking is a classic example. When people smoke, they take a break and breathe deep, often in the company of others they trust. When they try to quit smoking, they deprive themselves of these breaks. What if you took the break and the breaths and the company without the cigarette? Designing a smoke-free break makes it easier to quit, but most people forget to reward themselves with free time.

We resist free time because it feels weird at first. Your brain goes to dark places when you are suddenly free. This is why people strive to stay busy, as much as they complain about it. They only take breaks in the context of a habit that keeps their mind busy. You can free yourself of that habit if you practice the skill of taking unstructured time. It's scary at first when anxiety rushes in to fill the vacuum. But with practice, you will be able to avoid dark places without the pressure of external demands.

"I have no free time," you may insist. Your life seems like an endless stream of obligation. This is a circuit you built from experience. Maybe you were rewarded for looking busy when you were young, or punished for taking a break. That wired you to expect calamity if you take a break today. You can replace that circuit with a new one focused on the value of recharging your metabolic batteries.

8. DO ONE THING DIFFERENT

Anxiety surges when you feel like you've tried everything. You have nowhere to turn, so you feel trapped. Of course you haven't tried everything because you only try things you expect to work. Such expectations are limited by past experiences, so what if you tried something you did *not* expect to work? If that fails, you can try something else that you don't expect to work.

For example, if you are locked in an anxiety-provoking conflict with someone at work or at home, you may insist that the person needs to change because you have tried everything. But you have no power over the other person. You only have power over yourself. If you do one thing different, the whole situation might change. If it doesn't, you can do one other thing different.

This may seem foolish because the changes you can make are so small. It feels even more foolish to do something you don't expect to work. It feels dangerous too, as you imagine the criticism you would get for not "knowing what you're doing." A better way to look at it is that you know something will work, but you don't know what. So you experiment. And instead of judging by immediate results, you make small investments and monitor the returns.

We are used to hearing advice mongers insist on right answers and point fingers of ridicule at those who do otherwise. You may have pointed fingers yourself. We end up believing that right answers exist, and wrong answers are very risky. You run out of options quickly with such limits. You are stuck if you believe these limits are imposed on you by the external world. When you realize they are imposed by your fears, you can give yourself permission to try one thing different—even if you don't know why it should work.

This tool is most valuable when you are in a conflict with another person. You can't predict what will work because you can't see the world through the other person's lens. But if you do something different, your adversary is likely to do something different as well. If not, then try another thing different. Your power to experiment frees you from the feeling that the other person controls your destiny. When you take a minute to define what you want, you can find a way to meet your needs despite the tribulations of others.

9. RECIPROCITY

Reciprocity is the social glue of the mammal world. If you pick bugs out of someone's fur, it helps you get the bugs out of yours. If you admire someone's artwork, someone is likely to admire yours. When you want to cry into your beer, the way to get heard is to listen to someone else do the same. That can leave you in a puddle, but then you can find an exercise buddy, an addiction-recovery buddy, and a career-advancement buddy.

Reciprocity is not appropriate when it violates the rule of the law. Waiting your turn is better than bribing the maitre d'. Doing your own homework is better than cooperative cheating. I've lived in countries where bribery was the norm for traffic violations and public services. When I returned home, I was grateful for the rule of law. We benefit when our surgeons and pilots are accountable to standards rather than to private deal making. We are all challenged to manage our mammalian reciprocity impulse in healthy ways.

Research shows that wild baboons are curiously skilled at tallying favors given and received. They make careful decisions about which group members' fur to groom. Sometimes they are disappointed, but they focus on their next step. Reciprocity helps a mammal invest in options with good potential reward. You may think it's wrong to do something because you expect something in return. You have been told to give freely and expect nothing. But your inner baboon is keeping track, and it is not happy. Anxiety results when your verbal brain snubs your inner baboon. Accepting your mammalian urge for reciprocity helps you navigate between the extremes of isolation on the one hand and enmeshment on the other.

For example, when you groom others who don't groom you back, you have the power to make new choices. And when others groom you, you can think carefully about their expectations. This sounds obvious, but we are all biased by past experience. We have all had our expectations of reciprocity disappointed. Often we overreact in order to protect ourselves from future disappointments. When you know that reciprocity is natural, it's easier to recalibrate.

10. BUDGET YOUR ENERGY

When you are exhausted, cortisol is triggered and everything looks bad. Prospects look brighter when you are rested, but you can't save everything for those moments, because there aren't enough of them.

If you budget your energy, you can do more with less anxiety. You can do the hardest tasks when your energy is high, and save the easier tasks for lower moments. Once again, this sounds obvious but it's rarely done. One reason is that every task seems hard. Another is that we instinctively do the fun tasks first. Finally, we let others decide when we do which task. You can overcome these factors and spend your energy in a way that feels good.

Though you think each task is hard, there are tasks you dread and tasks you look forward to. It's tempting to do the pleasant tasks first, but that depletes your energy by the time you get to the dreaded ones. Instead, you could start each day with your hardest chore, and then flow easily toward the more desirable ones. That may seems hard at first, but if you make a habit of cracking one tough nut every morning, it will start to feel good. Do not expect yourself to crack tough nuts all day. Save your yuckiest challenges for the first thing in the morning, and only tackle one a day. It feels great to know your day will not be one yucky thing after another, and it feels great to know that five big threats will be out of the way five days from now.

If you try to tackle all the tough challenges at once, you run out of energy and everything seems hopeless. That motivates you to avoid tough challenges entirely. Budgeting your energy makes it possible to tackle tough challenges at a sustainable pace. With each nut you crack, you build the circuit that expects to succeed. Celebrate each nut you crack, but be sure you actually crack the nut before you celebrate.

Maybe you think this is impossible because your tough nuts are endless. You can break tough challenges into smaller chunks and tackle one chunk each morning. You can build pleasure into some tasks, and save them for your off-peak energy. Think carefully about how much you enjoy each task and when you choose to do it. Remember that a lion can only prevail in the hunt when it runs on peak energy. It would starve if it frittered its energy in all directions. A lion survives because it budgets its energy.

Sleep is a critical component of your energy budget. Your intelligent cortex needs plenty of sleep in order to have power over your mammal brain. You'll sleep better if you avoid stressful tasks in the evening. It may be tempting to get "one more thing" done, but you are robbing the time from tomorrow's energy budget.

Your personal life benefits from energy budgeting as much as your work life. There are dreaded tasks in your personal life and fun tasks. The un-fun things must get done in order to get the rewards you seek. To have a date on the weekend, you have to face the challenge during the week. To enjoy the holidays with family, you have to make nice with them today. To enjoy a new technology, you have to endure start-up costs. You may never tackle these tough challenges if you save them for the end of the day when you're exhausted. Invest some prime time in them instead.

When you have an especially yucky task, you might want to schedule a fun task right after it. Your enthusiasm will rise because you know you will soon be doing something fun. Apply this principle in the opposite direction too: when you have an especially fun task on your schedule, tackle an unpleasant chore just before it. Then you will get a tough challenge out of the way and still be sure your spirits are lifted in the end. If you have fun plans for lunch, crack a tough nut before lunch. But when you have a stressful lunch on your calendar, do a fun task before and after. Plan ways to recover your sense of well-being when it dips. You can prevent a cortisol spiral by sprinkling your pleasant tasks more strategically.

11. PREPARE YOUR FUN LIST IN ADVANCE

Most people have a chore list but not a fun list. You think fun should come naturally. But when anxiety turns on, healthy fun is hard to find. Every movie you check out looks bad. Every book you pick up seems boring. Every friend you call disappoints. It's helpful to prepare a fun list for moments like that.

When I reach the end of a hard day, I want relaxing entertainment, but it's hard for me to find things I like. I might have to scan lots of movies or books before one seems appealing. I don't feel like doing all that when I'm tired, but if I just watch the first thing I stumble on, I may hate it and get into a negative spiral. So I've learned to prepare a list in advance. Then, uplifting content is easy to find when I need it.

When I say "uplifting," I don't mean "educational." I don't mean that it makes me a better person in the eyes of others. I mean that it actually feels good. Your verbal brain may have one idea about content while your mammal brain has another. If you ignore your mammal brain, your fun time could add to your anxiety instead of taming it. Honor your mammal brain and it will take you where you want to go.

I am not always right about the content on my list. Sometimes I sit down with a movie or a book and find it distressing or boring. When this happens, I put it down and pick up something else. I have to make good use of my playtime in order to have energy for my work time.

I am always listening to an uplifting audiobook or podcast while exercising, driving, or doing household chores. This gives me extra fun time that I look forward to. Enjoying my downtime expands the energy I have to tackle the next morning's challenge.

Many people waste their fun time on content that stresses them. They allow negative messages to flood their brain while exercising and driving. We are gloriously free to choose our own content. Don't feed your brain with alarmism just because others do or because it's convenient. Find uplifting alternatives now so you always have a taming tool handy.

REMEMBER:

1. It's easy to wire yourself for unhealthy rewards because nature gives you a head start. But you can build new circuits to enjoy new rewards.

2. An activity that works mind and body together is an effective way to redirect your energy.

3. Mirror neurons activate when you see another individual get a reward or suffer pain. This activation makes it easier for you to initiate the steps needed to get that reward or avoid that harm yourself.

4. You can build anxiety-taming responses by finding tame people and observing them.

5. Variety helps you restore the pleasure that habituation diminishes. It's hard to try something new in a moment of distress, so start your exploring when you're feeling good.

6. Laughing is the sustainable way to get endorphin into your life. Humor is a sudden relief of perceived threat. When it's suddenly safe to lower your guard, tension is released in your *intrinsic muscles*. These muscles rarely get a workout so endorphin is released.

7. You can bring laughter into your life by viewing it as a strength, investing the time it takes to shop for it, and prioritizing your own sense of humor.

8. When a software engineer explains a complex coding problem to a rubber ducky, the solution usually comes fast. Though you feel like you've tried everything, explaining a problem out loud helps your verbal brain and your mammal brain work together in pursuit of a solution.

9. Self-expression helps you feel safe because it met your needs in youth. There is no perfect self-expression strategy. We all struggle to be heard in a world where everyone else is struggling to be heard. When you acknowledge your urge to be heard, you have power over this struggle instead of seeing it as a real external threat.

10. We often reward ourselves in unhealthy ways when what we really want is some downtime. People often resist taking a break because it has negative associations in their past. A free mind easily goes to dark places, but with practice, you learn to enjoy recharging your metabolic batteries.

11. You cannot predict what will please others, but you can try one thing different, and if it doesn't work, try something else. If you give yourself permission to experiment, you will always have options instead of feeling trapped.

12. Reciprocity is the social glue of the mammal world. You may think it's wrong to give with the expectation of a return, but your

inner mammal is always keeping score. It feels threatened when you ignore it. Reciprocity is not appropriate when it violates the rule of the law, so we are challenged to manage our mammalian reciprocity impulse in healthy ways.

13. Tackle one challenge each morning when your energy is highest. Challenges look worse later in the day when your energy is depleted. Do not expect yourself to tackle tough challenges all day. Break big challenges into smaller chunks. A lion can only survive by budgeting its energy, and its brain is designed to do that.

14. Uplifting content is hard to find. If you look for it when you're exhausted, you may give up and settle for negative content that triggers a spiral. Instead, prepare a list in advance. Then, you will always have a taming tool handy instead of feeding your brain with alarmism.

8

AVOID THESE SIX PITFALLS

You feel like a victim when you deny your own mammalian impulses.
You are better off seeing yourself as a protagonist.

Here are some troubleshooting tips to help you manage common obstacles on the path to taming anxiety. These pitfalls are natural, but when you know how to conquer them, you'll be super-natural.

1. THE MISSED EXIT PITFALL

"Half the pizza was gone by the time I thought about it." This comment came from a person struggling with eating habits, but you may have the same struggle with a different habit. You intend to choose a new road, but somehow you miss the exit. By the time you realize it, you're far down the old road. How can you jolt your attention sooner?

I tackled this problem when I moved to a new house and literally missed my exit a few times. It was a big deal because I taught night classes so I drove late at night. I'd get on the old road by accident and there was no safe place to turn around. I'd curse myself, but the next night I would do it again.

I realized that the sight of the old exit triggered my automatic pilot. So even though I knew what I was doing when I got in the car, I'd be on automatic by the time I reached the trigger. I needed a way to jolt my attention in that moment. So I designed the new habit of getting into the far left lane as soon as I got on the road. Then I would have to cross three lanes of traffic before I could exit. This was not part of my automatic circuit, so it was enough to jolt me into saying, "What am I doing?"

You can design a way to jolt yourself out of automatic pilot. The most famous example is hiding snack foods to make them hard to get to. Another well-known example is counting to ten before you unleash your venom. It doesn't always work, alas. Sometimes, your anxiety reaches full force before you remember your new plan. You need a way to snag your attention sooner. Here is a simple strategy.

Imagine that you are trying to reduce your coffee consumption. You plan an alternative feel-good ritual to replace your second and third cup of coffee. Before you put that plan into action, you need to build an exit ramp between your old habit and your new one. One week before your start date, notice when you think about getting coffee. Each time you think of it, stand up and spin around in a circle. Yes, literally stand up and spin. It feels foolish, but you'll do it because you want the coffee. The awkwardness of the gesture builds a marker in your brain that helps you notice your urge for a coffee. At first you may not notice until the cup is in your hand, but soon you will notice the urge before you act on it. Whenever you notice, stand up and spin. If you are at work, you can substitute a different awkward gesture that's less visible, like tapping your elbows behind your back. Any unusual behavior will put a wedge between the thought and the action, expanding your opportunity to activate a new response.

This strategy may sound like the concept of "triggers" in addiction recovery. There's an important difference, however. Recovering addicts are taught to identify their triggers so they can choose an alternative before it's too late. That strategy is useful, but it often leads to blame. You may blame externals for "triggering" you instead of discovering your own impulses. When you understand your impulses, you can find new ways to satisfy them instead of feeling deprived.

Anxiety flows from your automatic pilot. You don't intend to go there, but before you know it a small irritant stirs up a big response. You can build an exit ramp to leave that road sooner. Spin in a circle every time you notice anxiety. Whether it's tension in your body or words in your mind or triggers around you, stand up and spin. You will build a pathway that notices anxiety sooner, and gives you more time to exit to the new path you've planned.

2. THE MEDICAL DIAGNOSIS PITFALL

Anxiety has become a medical diagnosis. If you identify with this diagnosis, there are benefits. There's dopamine when you expect the health care system to meet your needs. There's serotonin when you gain a special status. There's oxytocin when you build community with fellow sufferers. There's cortisol relief when you feel like you can "do something."

But you pay a high price for these rewards. Embracing the medical view of anxiety undermines your belief in your own power. When you expect the health care system to "fix" you, you are not focused on building new pathways.

The disease view of emotions is hard to resist. If everyone else says troubling emotions are a disease, it's hard to think otherwise. And it's hard to pass up the dopamine, serotonin, oxytocin, and cortisol relief stimulated by the disease model. It's not surprising that the disease mind-set is so popular.

It helps to take a historical perspective on troubling emotions. For most of human history, you had to manage your emotions to tackle the immediate threat of hunger and predators. And you needed group ties to survive, so you honored group norms. If you failed to manage your emotions, evil spirits were presumed to be at work. Shamans were relied on to do something about those spirits. If the shaman failed, it was easy to blame the shaman or the evil spirits.

Then the ancient Greeks came along and blamed negative emotions on a black-bile imbalance. Ancient Chinese and Hindu philosophers blamed similar physiological imbalances. Now you could do something to restore balance. Healers could help, but you had some ownership.

Western science went on to cure diseases with medicine, surgery, and public health programs. We learned to expect science to cure troubling emotions as well. Advances in genetics strengthened trust in the disease model.

The medical model treats troubling emotions as symptoms, just as it would see physical pain as a symptom of cancer or tooth decay. This makes you a passive recipient of treatment instead of a manager of your brain. If you question this view, you are vilified by its proponents. Few people want to risk being vilified, so the disease view is widely embraced. You don't believe in evil spirits, but you blame emotions on external causes of one sort or another. You may even feel offended by the idea that you are creating your internal state. Health care providers cannot risk offending people. Teachers and public officials cannot risk offending people. Friends and family avoid offending. So you may not find a lot of support for taking responsibility for your emotions. But you benefit when you take responsibility regardless of what others think.

Getting help is valuable as long as you don't see it as a substitute for managing your emotions. You can think of "help" as an alliance rather than a rescue. This is hard to do when troubling emotions arise because it's easier to criticize the help than to blaze a new trail in your brain. Everyone else is criticizing the help, so that path is well developed.

Prevention is always better than treatment. If you have cancer or tooth decay, every treatment option has its down side. It's the same for mental health. My dentist has a sign that says, "Nothing the dentist can do will undo what the patient won't do." Help is nice, but self-care is essential.

However, when a horse is out of control, a rider is tempted to turn over the reins to anyone who promises to manage it. When your horse seems out of control, it's tempting to hand over the reins as well. Here is another way to think about it. Imagine yourself as a rodeo rider (or a competitor in the Equestrian Olympics if you prefer). Your horse had great trainers and you had great coaches, but once the event starts, it's just you and the horse. To win, you must work with your horse to navigate the obstacles in front of you, one after another. You will lose if your attention gets diverted to critiquing the preparation you got from your trainers and coaches. But whether you win or lose, you enjoy working with your horse.

I grew up before the disease model caught on. I'm not saying earlier models were better. My mother told me her anxiety was my fault. That explanation of anxiety was hard for my little brain to make sense of. It didn't feel true, and yet I had no other model. I urgently wanted to relieve my mother's anxiety because she let me feel it so deeply. But I couldn't figure out how I was turning it on so I could turn it off. While I was focused on her feelings, I ignored my own. Restraining my feelings helped protect me from her wrath. That is not the preferred way to learn self-control, and it flies in the face of the "let it all hang out" movement. But over the years, I recognized the benefits that accrued from my early training in self-control. I wonder where I'd be today if I had learned the disease view of emotions instead.

Once I left home, I searched for a better explanation of human emotions. In my twenties, I discovered Albert Ellis, the pioneer of Cognitive Behavioral Therapy. He held Friday-night workshops near my home that were fun and inexpensive. Ellis talked a lot about low frustration tolerance (LFT), and aimed to help people build higher frustration tolerance. I was glad to hear that healthy emotions were skills that can be built rather than effortless endowments. Ellis taught tools for managing troubling emotions instead of talking about disease.

It's hard to leave the disease view once you are in it. You lose oxytocin when you question it, as fellow anxiety sufferers stop seeing you as an ally and may condemn you as an enemy. You lose serotonin as you become an average person rather than a special person. You lose dopamine when you stop expecting a fix from the next doctor visit. In the short run, it may feel better to see yourself as a victim of bad health care. But in the long run, the disease view of emotions leaves you with a lot of cortisol.

3. THE BULLETPROOF ARMOR PITFALL

We are born vulnerable, so it's natural to want protection from an unsafe world. Seeking protection is a primal impulse, and finding protection feels so good that it wires you to expect more good feelings in that way. When self-protection feels good, it wires you for more of that. Self-protection gives you a reliable way to relieve threats. Repetition builds a pathway that makes it automatic. It's your handy personal armor.

Armor comes in many forms.

Muscle tension is a common variety because it's the mammal brain's natural threat response. Tension literally armors your body to protect you from anticipated harm. Even when you anticipate verbal harm or social harm, your mammal brain triggers tension.

Boredom is another common type of armor. It's your inner mammal's way of saying, "Don't get excited. There's nothing here for you. No rewards are expected, so don't invest anything."

Distraction is also a kind of armor. It relieves threatened feelings by sending your electricity in a new direction. Addictions are armor too, because they distract so effectively.

Other varieties of armor are perfectionism, anger, procrastination, resentment, sarcasm, defensiveness, and apathy. All of these thought habits put you in the one-up position, which makes you feel protected in the short run. They can hurt you in the long run, of course, and the hurt can trigger more self-armoring. Each brain relies on the circuits it has, which makes it hard to see how your armor is hurting you.

Armor has value, but it weighs you down. It's hard to take armor off once you put it on. But you can take it off and enjoy a new lightness and flexibility.

The first step is to notice your psychic armor. To do that, remember the time you told yourself, "I will never let this happen again." That is when you wired in the habit of defending yourself with whatever was available at that time. You will recognize your armor if you take time to ponder the pain of your myelin years. That is not an appealing project, of course. Do it in a quiet moment rather than during a cortisol surge, and plan something fun to do afterward. Start by thinking about a bad feeling you experienced recently, and trace it back to an early experience that fits the same pattern. When you find the match, celebrate your adult power instead of reliving the vulnerability of childhood.

The second step is to build confidence in your unarmored self. You can face the world's slings and arrows without it. Pain may result, but you will learn that pain doesn't kill you. Your brain is designed to anticipate pain, and you may be confusing anticipated pain with actual pain. You end up with a lot of extra pain. When you stop fearing pain, you stop creating the extra.

We have all experienced the pain of criticism and rejection in youth. We fear the loss of social bonds that protect us, and, truth be told, we fear the loss of the one-up position. These social threats feel like survival threats when you are safe from the more urgent threats of hunger and predation. We don't consciously see our disappointed dreams of grandeur as survival threats. And we don't consciously expect to relieve them with anger, boredom, perfectionism, procrastination, defensiveness, apathy, resentment, or addiction. But when a self-protective thought relieves the sting of social pain, it feels good, so your mammal brain goes there again.

It's natural to want armor when you're a hairless ape with a big cortex. It's hard to bear the thought of your own defenselessness. We can manage our armor more effectively when we are honest about it. We can build new protective skills instead of just repeating the ones built by accidents of youth. You can think of your new skills as hi-tech armor that's light and flexible. You can feel safe without the arsenal you built in the past.

4. THE SOCIAL COMPARISON PITFALL

Social comparison causes much human misery, yet we keep comparing ourselves to others. The mammal brain compares and reacts because that promotes survival. You have power over this impulse when you understand it. The mammal brain sees the strength of others as a survival threat. You don't intend to think that way, but your brain keeps comparing and releasing cortisol when you fall short. If you don't know you're doing this, you believe other people are putting you down or trying to dominate you. When you understand your brain, you know that you long for social dominance just like other mammals. This is why you give your attention to social comparisons.

It's hard to believe that animals engage in social comparison. We've been taught that animals are caring and sharing, and "our society is the problem." It's important to know the rest of the story. When two animals meet, each brain quickly makes a comparison and decides whether it's in the position of strength or the position of weakness. It makes a dominance gesture if it thinks it is stronger, and a submission gesture if it sees itself as weaker. If both individuals think they're stronger, a fight may erupt. Most of the time, fights are avoided because the weaker individual backs down. Animals are highly motivated to avoid pain.

Mammals get along once the uncomfortable business of status is resolved. They even cooperate in the face of a common enemy. But they care intensely about status because it affects the survival of their genes. The dominant individual is understood to have first access to any resources that come along. This is the mammalian way of preventing fights over food and mating opportunity. Weaker individuals restrain their impulses in the presence of a stronger individual. The dominant animal may share resources and control aggression once it has the position of dominance because that is what matters. The brain built by natural selection rewards you with a good feeling when you come out on top.

The mammal brain is skilled at assessing its strength relative to others because survival depends on it. Young monkeys spend a lot of time wrestling, which trains their brains to compare their strength to others. When you were young, you spent a lot of time comparing your strengths to others. In adolescence, you added new social comparisons to those circuits. Your mirror neurons influenced your choice of traits to compare. You eagerly noticed which traits brought rewards and which traits brought pain. You wired yourself to expect rewards from certain strengths and to feel threatened by certain weaknesses. You ended up with pathways that tell you when you're in the weaker position and need to back down, and when you're in the position of advantage.

These pathways are well-myelinated from repeated use. They easily stimulate good feelings when you gain an advantage and bad feelings when your status is threatened. But you have always been told not to think this way, so you learn to ignore your internal impulses and blame externals. You believe your own spin because you do not decide in words to make social comparisons. But words are not needed for a mammal to make social comparisons. All it takes is chemicals and pathways built from experience with those chemicals.

It's better not to compare, of course. We want everyone to be equal. When you say this with your verbal brain, you get respect and acceptance.

But your mammal brain is still comparing. The more equal people are, the harder your brain looks for differences in order to make status distinctions. Bill Gates's sneakers differ little from yours in the context of human history, but your inner mammal notices the difference and it cares.

The bigger a creature's brain, the more complex its social comparisons. For example, reptiles compare in a simple way. When a reptile sees a critter bigger than itself, it runs. When it sees a smaller critter, it tries to eat it. And when it sees something about the same size, it tries to mate it. Reptiles don't live in groups because they can't restrain conflict among bigger and smaller individuals. Mammals inherited the brains of reptiles and added on. Mammals evolved the capacity for strength in numbers by using social comparison to prevent conflict.

Smaller-brained mammals compare in simpler ways. For example, when a bovine joins a new herd, it fights each individual once, and thus wires itself to "know its place." It will not update its status perceptions unless there's a major shake-up. Monkeys, with their larger cortex, are continually challenging and renegotiating their status. A monkey even recognizes the relative status of two other monkeys to each other. Status-seeking monkeys made more copies of their genes, so status-seeking brains got passed on.

A mammal compares itself to others before reaching for food or mating opportunity, so social comparison is effectively more primal than food or sex. It's hard to think about animals this way. We prefer to imagine them in a pristine state of altruism. But when you know the truth, you can discover your primal impulses and escape from their grip. You can notice yourself making social comparisons at work, at the gym, at parties, and on your screen. You can notice the feelings these comparisons trigger. You can design a healthier alternative and repeat it until your electricity flows there.

So what is a healthy alternative? Each time you catch yourself comparing, you can tell yourself: "My mammal brain wants the one-up position because that feels safe. My mammal brain sees stronger individuals as a threat. I am creating these feelings by making comparisons." When you say this to yourself, you can manage your feelings instead of jumping to the conclusion that you are under attack. When you fail to get the one-up position, you can reassure your inner mammal that your survival is not actually threatened.

There is no simple solution. If you seek the one-up position all the time, you end up with a lot of conflict. If you submit all the time, you get a lot of cortisol and little serotonin. Our only choice is to make constant decisions about when to assert and when to let go. Fortunately, that's the job our brain evolved to do. We can do it with less intensity by reminding ourselves that the life-or-death feelings are just chemicals triggered by old pathways.

You may still be saying "I don't do this." You see others doing it, especially people you hate. But when it comes to yourself and your allies, you are sure you are above all that. Yet you often believe "they" are putting you down, so you have no choice but to respond. You feel like a victim when you deny your own mammalian impulses. You are better off seeing yourself as a protagonist.

For most of human history, these frustrations were managed with rigid rules. It's fascinating to know that many human languages have status distinctions built in. For example, you cannot speak Spanish or Japanese without designating the listener as above you or below you. When I speak Spanish, I get anxious about this choice. When I use the form with more respect I fear being too formal, and when I opt to be informal I fear being disrespectful. I might be more relaxed about it if I were a native speaker, but then I would be still making status distinctions. I would just be doing it on autopilot.

We don't like to talk about our animal urge for social importance, yet we have many words to denote it: pride, ego, confidence, competitiveness, status, assertiveness, dignity, and ambition. We call it getting respect, attention, or recognition, and feeling special, important, or appreciated. Harsh words come to mind when we think about our rivals' quest for social advantage, while our own quest feels like an innocent survival necessity.

The pain of social comparison is intensified by our brain's natural focus on the strengths of others. For example, when I meet a certain friend, my eye instantly notices a waist that is much thinner than mine. She instantly notices that my hair is much thicker than hers. I feel bad about my thick waist, while I take my thick hair for granted. She feels bad about her thin hair, and takes her thin waist for granted. We are both focused on our weaknesses rather than our strengths. We are both stimulating unhappy chemicals rather than happy chemicals.

What if we did the opposite? What if I focused on traits I felt good about, and she focused on traits she felt good about? At first, focusing on your strengths can feel rude, conceited, arrogant. The word "self-satisfied" has come to be used as an insult. Focusing on your strengths feels dangerous too, because monitoring your weakness keeps you safe. If I stopped worrying about my waist it might get bigger and bigger. If my friend stopped worrying about her hair it may get thinner. It's easy to see how we end up focused on our weaknesses, putting ourselves down and then resenting others for doing it to us. But we have the power to focus on our strengths and release that resentment.

5. THE HIGH-SCHOOL BRAIN PITFALL

Puberty brings myelin that paves neural pathways. Each brain filters experience through a lens built in adolescence. This is why life often feels like a high school cafeteria.

You may not remember the adolescent experiences that are shaping your neurochemistry today. Your brain just relies on the pathways it has.

It helps to know that "high school brain" afflicts everyone. You can be less harsh with yourself and others when you know how it works.

Sex is just part of the adolescent equation. The mammal brain evolved to reward "reproductive success," which includes everything that comes before and after sex. Before sex is the quest for a partner, and after sex is the quest to keep the young alive. No conscious intent to reproduce is involved. Animals are not consciously trying to spread their genes, but their brain rewards them with a good feeling when they take steps that promote their genes. Natural selection built a brain that responds vigorously to everything that affects your ability to find a partner and protect children. This is why your chemicals are so affected by an inviting smile or a career boost, and why a bad hair day can feel like a survival threat.

"Popularity" in high school is curiously linked to the factors that promote reproductive success in monkeys: a healthy appearance, a network of social alliances, and a willingness to take risks. Steps toward these factors trigger reward chemicals in young brains, thus wiring adolescents to seek more of that. Whatever works tells the brain, "This is the way to go." If you look closely at the woes and joys of your adolescence, you will find a remarkable correspondence with your woes and joys today.

It's easy to ridicule high school brain in others, but if you are honest, you can see that ridiculing others puts you in the one-up position. Ridicule is an adolescent way to enjoy a moment of social dominance. It's not surprising that ridicule is so pervasive, but you can learn to notice and redirect this impulse.

You can learn to recognize the high school template in your interpretation of today's events. Then you can train yourself to stop and generate an alternative when you start slipping into high school brain. A new pathway will build, and your new view will light up more easily.

6. THE HELL-IN-A-HANDBASKET PITFALL

When you tell yourself "things are going to hell in a handbasket," you stimulate cortisol. The hell feels real because the cortisol is real. You can relieve cortisol by replacing your "hell in a handbasket" template with a more positive mind-set.

Hell-in-a-handbasket thinking is popular because it feels good in the short run. It stimulates oxytocin with the image that we're all in the handbasket together. It stimulates serotonin by suggesting that your knowledge is superior. It stimulates dopamine by helping you predict rewards. It relieves cortisol by distracting you from private distress with its focus on public distress. These good feelings wire you to return to the hell-in-a-handbasket mind-set in future moments of distress.

Of course, it feels bad to think things are going downhill. So you end up with cortisol in the long run when you rely on this mind-set for short-run relief. It's not surprising that escapism is often allied with hell-in-a-handbasket thinking. Why not have another drink if everything is falling apart?

You do not consciously want to think this way. But when anxiety strikes, you urgently want to "do something" and you don't always know what to do. Any reliable alternative is appreciated. You observe the relief strategies of others and their hell-in-a-handbasket thinking is palpable. Your mirror neurons take it in. After a while, the declinist world view feels obviously true because the flow is so effortless.

People have bonded around a shared sense of threat throughout human history. Children learn about expected threats from elders, and the expectation gets wired in. If you reject shared expectations, you risk being seen as stupid or "not one of us."

Every historical era has its way of explaining threatened feelings. Every era has its high priests who define shared threats for others. High priests must compete for public attention in order to sustain their status. They do that by designing messages that are popular and by challenging rival high priests. Today, academics and mass media define shared threats for us. If you reject their message of decline, you risk being seen as stupid or "not one of us."

The human cortex is designed to find patterns in the external world that match patterns in your neurons. It's easy to find external evidence of decline because the inputs flow so easily into neural pathways created by declinist expectations. Others do it too, so it seems like absolute proof. But when you know how your brain works, you can see how the declinist pattern is constructed and build yourself an alternative. Your world will suddenly look different.

I am not suggesting that you replace the hell-in-a-handbasket view with a heaven-is-around-the-corner view. That is not really different. It's still relying on a preconceived pattern to predict rewards and pain.

So what is the alternative?

Stop blaming the world for your feelings and notice how you create them. This doesn't mean blaming yourself. You can practice self-acceptance. You are a mammal with a big cortex. You urgently want to survive, yet you know you are mortal. You want to spread your unique individual essence but you don't always prevail. You enjoy social trust, yet common enemies are what spark it. These impulses are easy to see in others. When you see them in yourself, you have power.

REMEMBER:

1. Your new tame pathway is only useful if you exit from your old anxiety pathway in a timely manner. You can build an exit ramp that helps you do that. Make an awkward physical gesture when you notice the urge you want to change, and you will build a pathway that helps you flow into your new choice.

2. The disease view of emotions is historically new. It rewards you with a sense of community, an expectation of reward, and a sense of being special. But in the end, learning to manage your horse benefits you more than giving the reins to someone else.

3. Self-protection is like armor—it helps you feel safe, but it weighs you down and it's hard to take off. Well-known varieties of psychic armor are muscle tension, boredom, anger, perfectionism, and procrastination. You can feel light and flexible if you take off your armor. To build confidence in your unarmored self, practice distinguishing real pain from anticipated pain, and real survival threats from anticipated survival threats.

4. Social comparison causes misery because the mammal brain sees the strength of others as a survival threat. When you ignore your mammalian urge for social dominance, you believe others are putting you down. When you understand your mammal brain, you see that you are a participant in mammalian social rivalry and creating your own feelings about it.

5. Puberty brings myelin which paves neural pathways, so the experiences of adolescence build the lens through which we see the world. Natural selection built a brain that responds vigorously to everything that affects your ability to find a partner and protect children. No conscious intent to reproduce is necessary for our chemicals to respond to the variables that promote reproductive success, such as a healthy appearance, a network of social alliances, and a willingness to take risks.

6. The hell-in-a-handbasket mind-set is popular because it triggers good feelings: that you know what is going on, and that we're all in the handbasket together. Expectations of decline feel true because they're socially reinforced and because the cortex finds evidence that fits expectations. But hell-in-a-handbasket thinking feels bad in the long run. When you know you are creating it, you can create an alternative.

9

FOOD AND ANXIETY

A nap would give you a boost, but that seems impossible. A call from the lover who dumped you last year would give you a boost, but that seems impossible. A brownie is possible.

Hunger was a huge threat for most of human history. Our brain is good at looking for food because that relieves the threat. When you are anxious, you may find yourself looking for food. Then you may get anxious about what you eat. This thought loop can ensnare you. One minute you're longing for something to nibble on, and the next minute you're fearing the consequences. This chapter helps you escape that loop. We'll see how food stimulates the happy brain chemicals, and how you can redirect yourself toward new ways to stimulate them.

Food triggers dopamine, serotonin, oxytocin, and endorphin, which is why it's so motivating. When you understand these motives, you can enjoy the good feelings without overeating.

This chapter is not aimed at weight loss. It aims to tame anxiety. But since eating is both a cause of anxiety and an effect, it may help you step toward new eating habits. We must understand our natural food impulses in order to manage them, so let's start with a close look at why our brain responds so intensely to food.

WHY WE'RE SO FOCUSED ON FOOD

Watch monkeys at the zoo and you will see that they're constantly looking for food. They are not even hungry, because zookeepers feed them, but their eyes are constantly scanning the ground for potential snacks (both insects and leftovers). Sometimes they see another monkey score, which increases their vigilance. A bit before feeding time, they shift their vigilance to the door where their meal will appear. I used to lead zoo tours and would tell people to think of these monkeys when they find themselves in front of the refrigerator wondering how they got there. Zoos are not a perfect reflection of natural behavior, but if you could see chimpanzees in the wild, you would see even more excitement about food.

We care about food because it works. It really does boost your peak power. Research shows that people make better decisions when their blood glucose isn't low. When your blood glucose falls, you give in to temptation more easily. (This is known as *ego depletion*.) The problem is that once your blood glucose is back up to normal, you don't get additional power from additional food. But you expect to get it because you got it before. This is why you think of food when you need a boost.

Our brain is designed to focus on unmet needs. Food doesn't meet an unmet need if you've already eaten, so the relief value of food requires a bit of explaining. Let's say it's afternoon and you're dreaming of buying a brownie. You need a boost, and it's the best way you can think of to get it. A nap would give you a boost, but that seems impossible. A call from the lover who dumped you last year would give you a boost, but that seems impossible. A brownie is possible. So even though you're not really hungry, you get up and buy a brownie. And it works! The act of getting and eating the brownie interrupts the thought pattern you were having when you started dreaming of it. The threat you were imagining is gone, if only for a few minutes. This teaches your brain that a brownie relieves threats.

Let's say you make good use of your break. You get back to work and tackle the problem that was worrying you. Hooray! But with that threat out of the way, your brain looks around for the next potential threat. You feel the brownie in your stomach and imagine it going to your arteries. You think about calories, additives, gluten, partially hydrogenated fat and high-fructose corn syrup. Your cortisol surges.

We evolved to see food as a reward, but today we often see it as a threat. You read about dietary health risks and hear scare talk from family and friends. Cortisol builds a pathway that triggers fear when you eat, or just think about eating.

Fear is an ancient regulator of food choices. Our ancestors lived in fear of running out of food before the next growing season. They feared food shortages due to drought or pestilence or war. Each bite they ate was one less bite that would be available in time of need. Our ancestors managed their food intake the way you might manage your water bottle on a long hike. You weigh the reward against the risk before you open your mouth. Today, we are less fearful of food shortages. We have replaced that fear with the fear of a suboptimal diet. Fear remains our guide because it's a powerful motivator of self-restraint. So, we have gone from scarcity to abundance without relaxing our fear. The challenge of the next generation is to eat sensibly with joy instead of with fear.

In a world of abundance, overeating is a real threat. To relieve it we must restrain the food-seeking urge that evolved in a world of scarcity. But self-restraint is a cortisol circuit built by fear of consequences. This leads to the predicament of cortisol-if-you-do and cortisol-if-you-don't. How can we make good food choices without constant fear?

You can enjoy your steps toward meeting your needs. You can maximize the pleasure of food when you're hungry and be prepared with other pleasures when you're not hungry. We've seen throughout this book that the happy chemicals are your brain's signal that a need has been met. You keep striving to stimulate them because it relieves the bad feeling that your survival is threatened. The more ways you can stimulate happy chemicals, the less tempted you are to overeat. Negativity about food is not the path to a healthy diet. You can preserve the pleasure of food and still tame the impulse to reward yourself with food. You can do it one happy chemical at a time.

THE DOPAMINE VALUE OF FOOD

The joy of food is one of your first experiences in life. A newborn baby enjoys a surge of dopamine when it first tastes milk. The baby doesn't know what milk is, or what nutritional needs are, but the brain releases dopamine when milk relieves low blood sugar. That builds a pathway that says, "This is the way to feel good! Get me more of this!"

But a baby doesn't know how to get it. The next time it is hungry, it surges with cortisol and crying is its only way to "do something." Then it hears a sound. Suddenly, its dopamine is triggered because that sound was heard during a prior dopamine release. So, at one day of age, a brain is already drawing on past experience to feel good. A baby expects to feel good when it hears its mother's voice, though it doesn't know why.

Whenever a bad feeling suddenly changes to a good feeling, it means you have relieved a threat and met a need at the same time. That builds a huge pathway because it's a huge survival boost. Huge pathways create the expectation that food will relieve your woes. If you fall and hurt yourself and someone gives you a cookie, it feels like cookies have magic powers.

Dopamine motivates steps toward food as much as it motivates eating itself. A huge investment of effort was necessary to get food in the past. The good feeling of dopamine motivated that effort. Our ancestors migrated to better hunting grounds and planted fruit trees because anticipated rewards triggered dopamine, which triggered action. Today, you may find it hard to get a parking spot near your favorite donut shop, and your dopamine surges when you see a place to park.

If you were a pioneer on the Oregon Trail and ate nothing but jerky and biscuits, you would be very motivated to reach the ripe berry bushes farther down the trail. Today, variety is so easily available that it's less exciting. Thus, we find other ways to stimulate the excitement of dopamine with food, such as cooking a dish that takes all day, reading restaurant reviews, planning holiday meals, scouting for rare ingredients, and growing vegetables. Watching cooking shows is an extremely popular option. These quests for food have no calories but they feel good because our brain evolved to forage. You may think food quests are a dangerous prelude to overeating, but this is often not true. Many Food Network fans have a healthy diet. We can find new sources of excitement to replace the excitement of noshing.

When I was young, I was always on a quest for new ice cream flavors. Travel in Europe thrilled me with new ice cream horizons. I didn't overeat; I just enjoyed the quest. But as the decades went by, I ran out of new flavors to discover. Then I learned that Europe has two-hundred-year-old cafe/pastry shops. This triggered my cream circuits and my history circuits and my travel circuits at the same time. I was thrilled to have a new quest to replace the old one, and planned a tour of the historic pastry shops of Vienna. When I got there, I spent a lot of time looking at the pastry before I chose one. I even photographed a lot of them. When I finally ordered a pastry, I cut it in quarters. I'd save half for the next day, and a quarter for dessert that night. I didn't have to overindulge because I was enjoying the quest. I most enjoyed the pastry at the cafe where Sigmund Freud had his breakfast and read his newspaper.

The joy of the quest makes more sense when you understand the difficulty of meeting food needs in the state of nature. You could not eat a nut unless you invested effort in gathering, shelling, and roasting them. You would not overeat because the investment of effort is more than the reward. Today you can eat shelled nuts out of a bag. The whole bag costs a tiny amount of labor to buy, even at minimum wage. You pop nuts into your mouth because it's a big reward for a small effort. The reward is minor if you're not hungry, but nuts have fat, protein, and salt that are rare in the state of nature. So, from your mammal brain's perspective, it's still a reward. The easy availability of food is the crux of today's challenge. This is widely overlooked because of the misguided belief that food comes effortlessly in the state of nature. The truth is that a huge share of energy went into meeting food needs in the past, which is why we have extra energy today.

We look for good ways to invest our energy because that's what our brain is designed to do. We evaluate these investments with pathways built from past experience. That's why baking bread is a reward to one person and a pain to another person. Maybe you feel rewarded by hiking to pick wild herbs or discussing at length the subtle qualities of a wine. Maybe not. It depends on the associations you have built in your past.

Our food fears are learned from experience as well. You have surely noticed that your food fears differ from the food fears of others. If you think about it, you can identify the experiences that created these fears.

Our dopamine responses have much in common despite our unique experiences. For example, variety stimulates dopamine. Our ancestors ate the same thing much of the time. When they had the chance to try a rare food, they became excited. Variety triggers dopamine because it helps satisfy unmet nutritional needs. You can stimulate dopamine with variety. You can increase the reward value of your breakfast by trying a new cereal or your salad by adding different ingredients. And I love to increase the reward value of beer by sampling a few different tiny beers.

Color also increases the reward value of food. In the statue of nature, color triggered dopamine because colorful foods were typically scarce and high in nutrients. Today we have learned to make our food colorful without artificial chemicals. Restaurants and cooking shows have learned to compete by emphasizing natural color. Assembling foods with attractive color has been elevated to such a high art that it has come to be known as "food porn." You can choose ingredients with visual appeal and enjoy more dopamine from less food.

If you don't make an effort to enjoy food in new ways, automatic impulses easily take hold. The first bite of a cookie feels so good that it builds a big circuit, inviting your electricity the next time you look for a way to feel good. But after a few bites, the thrill is gone and you worry about the consequences. The bad feeling sends you looking for another quick boost. This thought loop can make you miserable. Fortunately, food stimulates other happy chemicals, and this gives you other alternatives.

THE OXYTOCIN VALUE OF FOOD

Whatever triggered your oxytocin in youth built a pathway that turns it on today. Food is usually linked to that circuit because it's linked to your early social experience. If you enjoyed social trust around a table in youth, that will activate your sense of safety today. If your table was full of conflict, you have some different associations. Most of us have a combination of positive and negative associations for shared meals, which is why food can evoke social pain and the joy of belonging at the same time.

Every mammal seeks safety in numbers. If we count on food to trigger that feeling, we may eat too much. There are other ways to enjoy the sense of acceptance we naturally crave, but they're easy to forget when we expect to get it through food. Such expectations are reinforced by the images of shared meals we see around us. In the past that might have centered on village festivals and visits to relatives. Today, movies and media present images of convivial meals, and restaurant windows display them live. Your brain easily links food to social support.

The social solidarity of other times and places is widely idealized. The reality is that group meals were necessary before technology simplified food prep. People embraced alternatives to group meals as soon as they emerged. In our idealized image, mealtime meant sharing your deepest hopes and dreams and getting unconditional approval from everyone assembled. The reality was often quite different. Expectations were rigid, and if you failed to meet them you would be excluded from the shared meal. That meant hunger, so you kept your big ideas to yourself. When a gazelle eats with the herd, it gets poked by other gazelles, but it eats with the herd to avoid predators.

In our Hollywood images, meals are prepared with love, and crops are grown with love. Our illusions about collective eating are fueled by the cooperative farms celebrated in fiction and nonfiction. The bad news is often left out. Most cooperatives dissolve from conflict. Food preparation took a huge amount of drudge work in the past, and resentment was sometimes an ingredient. When you idealize the community of the past, you feel like your life is missing something. It helps to be realistic about the past.

When I visited Asia, a colleague invited me to a meal with her family. Everyone served themselves from platters in the center. My friend told me that everyone notices what everyone else takes, so you grow up learning to watch what you eat. I suddenly realized that shared meals had helped people restrain their food intake for most of human history. The end of that lifestyle brought two new challenges: finding new ways to build social trust, and finding new ways to restrain food intake. I was reminded of the moment in my first semester at college when I realized I could choose food without another person's judgment. We often long to free ourselves from the judgment of others, but then our survival depends on the quality of our own judgment.

You need social trust in your life, of course. In the past, your choices were limited, so you had to sustain trust with the people you had. Today, there are numerous options, but sustaining trust is still hard for any group of mammals. You can choose to build trust around food or to build it in other ways.

Your brain is longing for real trust, rather than fake trust. Real trust requires reciprocity over time. Sharing food can be a stepping stone to real trust, but it is not a substitute. The more you recognize your real oxytocin needs, the less you expect to meet them by eating.

THE SEROTONIN VALUE OF FOOD

Children sometimes fight over food the way monkeys do. By the time we reach adulthood, we learn to restrain that impulse, but the longing for power doesn't stop when you stop grabbing other people's bananas. We look for ways to stimulate that one-up feeling, and food often gets involved. Your mammal brain finds ways to be special and fill your belly at the same time.

Status food is an obvious example. Everyone has seen the iconic image of a wealthy big shot with a bib on, eating a lobster. Each generation creates its own food-based status symbols. In tribal societies, you would get status by providing a banquet for everyone you know. Such banquets were the only chance to eat meat for many people. When my mother was a child, meat was such a luxury that having a slice of ham in your cheese sandwich was a status symbol. Today, status foods come and go, but you know what they are.

In a world of food abundance, the biggest status indicator is being thin. Many people starve themselves to achieve this status. They enjoy the serotonin but starvation triggers constant cortisol.

Food can stimulate serotonin in many other ways. You may feel special when your diet is healthier than the average. If it's more ethical as well, you get extra bonus points.

The one-up feeling is also released when you can get others to honor your dietary preferences. Opposing the food habits of others does it too.

It's not surprising that people invest so much energy negotiating their food rules, whether in a family, a social group, or the public forum.

We don't like to acknowledge this aspect of food. We don't like to acknowledge the mammalian urge for social power at all. But serotonin rewards you with a good feeling when you get it, and your inner mammal feels threatened when you don't.

The quest for serotonin is hard for everyone because it's quickly metabolized, so you have to keep stimulating it. Also, your brain habituates to any status you have, so new and improved status is what it takes. This leaves us eager for one-up opportunities no matter where we are in life. And since we are eager for food as well, the two goals often overlap. Food creates frequent opportunities to assert yourself and feel important.

Yet every opportunity can lead to disappointment instead. No matter how slim your waistline, someone will have a slimmer one. No matter how perfect your dinner party, someone's will be better. No matter how ethical your diet, someone's will be more ethical, and however high your soufflé, someone's will be higher. Of course, these quests go too far sometimes, but you don't see that when you're in the grip of social comparison. Thus, the mammalian urge for social dominance can permeate your mealtime.

You may say you don't care about social dominance, but if you find yourself mindlessly shoveling snacks into your mouth, think about what happened in the last few hours. You will probably find that you have experienced a threat to your social dominance. We all struggle with the feeling of powerlessness because we are all born powerless. Food choices are a popular way to relieve those feelings of weakness. We do it in myriad ways, depending on our life experience. However you got wired, you can build new pathways to feel pride in good food choices without stewing over other people's food choices.

ENDORPHIN

Hot pepper triggers a bit of endorphin, but habituation means you have to eat hotter and hotter to stimulate it.

Chewing triggers a bit of endorphin, because it exercises your jaw muscles. The appeal of chewing gum or a nice bowl of popcorn rests in part on the endorphin. The historical significance of chewing is fascinating. Before the invention of cooking food, our ancestors had to spend a huge portion of their day chewing food to get enough nutrition. Chimpanzees spend a huge part of their day chewing. Elephants and gazelles spend almost their whole day chewing. Cooked food enabled humans to swallow more nutrition in less time, leaving us more time for other things. Today, it's nice to spend some of that time chewing.

Starving triggers endorphin too. It also triggers cortisol, of course. The joint neurochemical message effectively promotes survival in the state of nature. Cortisol alerts a forager to the urgency of its food needs, and endorphin masks hunger pain so it's easier to forage. Hunger only triggers endorphin when you're at the point of distress. And even then, you habituate, so it takes more distress to stimulate it. Starving for endorphin is thus dangerous and foolish and absolutely *not* recommended. It is only mentioned here for the sake of insight. We are designed to honor our natural urge to eat.

FOOD TRADE-OFFS

In this book we have seen that our brain makes constant trade-offs between rewards and pain. It also trades off one reward against another, and old reward pathways against new ones. You have more power over these trade-offs when you understand them. Food choices can help you recognize your thought habits because the rewards are tangible instead of being abstract.

Food seeking interrupts negative thought patterns, and that's a valuable tool in some situations. But if you rely on this tool too often, you do yourself harm. You must keep assessing the trade-offs to get what you want.

You can enjoy the reward value of food without overindulging. You can stop seeing food as a threat. When you understand the reward value of food, you can enjoy the rewards without adding to your anxiety. You are always doing this with the circuits you have, but with effort, you can build some new circuits.

When I was a kid, my mother brought us to an ice cream parlor for sundaes when report cards came out. Today, rewarding children with treats is considered bad, but I did not become a sundae junkie. I only have one or two a year, and only small sundaes after a big investment of effort, which is eerily similar to my early experience. Recently, I made a trip to my hometown after living three thousand miles away for a long time, and I was eager to check out the old ice cream parlor. As you may guess, it was a huge disappointment. The historic character was gone, including the metal dishes. I didn't consciously care about the metal dishes, but with each spoonful, I missed the familiar clink of metal against metal. This was a great reminder of the way our experience of food is shaped by old pathways.

When we understand the power of these old pathways, we can appreciate the effort it takes to build new ones.

REMEMBER:

1. Hunger was a huge threat for most of history, and our brain evolved to look for food to relieve the threat.
2. The good feeling of relief builds a pathway that expects relief from food even when you're not actually hungry.
3. People make worse decisions when their blood glucose falls. But once a bit of food brings your blood glucose back up to normal, you don't get additional power from additional food.
4. Historically, fear of food scarcity helped people restrain their urge to eat. In today's world of abundance, fear is likewise an effective motivator of restraint. The challenge of the next generation is to eat sensibly with joy instead of with fear.
5. You can learn to maximize the pleasure of food when you're hungry and be prepared with alternative pleasures when you're not hungry.
6. The good feeling of dopamine motivated our ancestors to migrate to better hunting grounds and to plant fruit trees. Higher expected rewards trigger more dopamine.
7. The excitement of noshing can be replaced by the excitement of zero-calorie food quests, such as watching cooking shows, growing vegetables, reading restaurant reviews, planning holiday meals, scouting for rare ingredients, or cooking something that takes all day. Variety and color stimulate dopamine too.
8. If you enjoyed social trust around a table in youth, that will activate your sense of safety today. Most of us have a combination of positive and negative associations for shared meals, which is why food can evoke social pain and the joy of belonging at the same time.
9. Your brain is longing for real trust rather than fake trust. Sharing food can be a stepping stone to real trust, but it is not a substitute. The more you recognize your real oxytocin needs, the less you expect to meet them by eating.
10. Food can stimulate your mammalian urge for social dominance in many ways. Every generation has its status food. And you may

enjoy a one-up feeling when your diet is healthier or more ethical than someone else's diet.

11. People invest a lot of energy negotiating food rules in a family, social group, or public forum, because social dominance stimulates serotonin.

12. Endorphin is triggered a bit by hot pepper and by chewing.

13. Food-seeking interrupts negative thought patterns, which is a valuable tool in some situations. But if you rely on it too often, you do yourself harm. Your brain is designed to keep assessing trade-offs to get what you want.

10

HELP OTHERS TAME ANXIETY

When you offer acceptance or respect to an angry or anxious person,
you feel like a good guy. When you withhold it, you risk being
branded a bad guy. Thus, you are really focused on your own needs
when you reward bad behavior, even as you invoke a higher purpose.
It takes a strong focus on long-term goals to transcend this impulse.

The urge to help others is strong, but your power to help others is limited. You cannot access the command center of someone else's brain. You can only help a person if that person activates the neurons. You can help others tame anxiety by

- talking to them about their inner mammal,
- modeling a desired behavior for their mirror neurons to receive, and
- rewarding the behavior you want, rather than the behavior you don't want.

This chapter is intentionally last because you shouldn't try to tame others until you have tamed yourself. It's tempting to start with others because it always feels like they are the cause of your anxiety. You think everything will be good when others change. This focus on others diverts you from the central task of finding your own power. Worst of all, blaming your anxiety on others teaches others to blame as well. So tame your own anxiety before you read on.

There are good reasons to want to help, of course. When someone you care for is suffering, you feel it. When your herd is happier, you are happier. And, truth be told, you feel important when you help someone, and that serotonin signal of social importance feels safe. You stimulate dopamine when you help someone because you approach rewards with them, and you stimulate oxytocin when it builds your sense of trust and belonging. Helping feels good.

Being honest about these motivations is important because "help" doesn't always help. Sometimes, we do things in the name of "help" that make things worse for the person we want to help. This chapter explores a better way to help. You can help others master their brain in the long run instead of just having feel-good moments in the short run.

You can help someone learn the three-step taming tool. But talking about the tool is not the same as using the tool. You know it was difficult to get it into your own brain, so you can appreciate the challenge for others. You can help them do it with talk, mirror neurons, and a careful use of carrots and sticks. Each of these has limited power, but used together they can help. Here's how to manage these tools, whether in a professional capacity or a personal capacity.

TALK, TALK, TALK

Telling an anxious person to relax doesn't help. Pointing out the bright side of a situation often fails too. Anxiety is hard to tame with words because it's hard to find the connection between the verbal brain and the chemical brain. It's like hearing a foreign language. When you hear a word in a language you don't speak, it has no meaning because you don't have a circuit connecting it to other experiences. A person needs the experience of feeling safe in order to evoke it with words. This leaves us with a chicken-and-egg problem: how can you help others activate a feeling they haven't lived?

You can help them find a new trail in their brain and activate it repeatedly. This is hard, like learning a foreign language. We don't know why it's hard to learn a new language, since we seemed to learn our native language effortlessly. In the same way, we learned our old emotional responses effortlessly, but new ones are curiously hard to learn. The truth is that early learning involved an enormous amount of repetition, and a lot of myelin. In adulthood, the myelin is gone, so repetition is even more important.

Anyone can learn new tame responses by repeating them a lot, but people are rarely eager to do this. When they don't learn quickly, they think something is wrong with them. It is very helpful for people to know that repetition is necessary for everyone.

Learning a new emotional response is harder than learning a new word. You can associate a new word with an old meaning, but you may not have an association for a new emotion. Your electricity doesn't flow there if the neurons aren't connected. You can help a person make new connections by activating nearby circuits. For example, this book has used animal analogies to help access impulses that we rarely put into words. You can design analogies and word pictures that are meaningful to the person you are trying to help. However they have experienced confidence in their own steps in the past, you can help them find and reactivate those circuits.

Breaking abstractions into smaller chunks is another way to help a person activate a new circuit. For example, when two fishermen talk to each other about their day, they can say a lot in a few words because they have a shared vocabulary. When they talk to non-fishermen, they have to break things down into concepts that are familiar to people. It's the same when you explain the concept of feeling safe to a person who does not feel safe. You break the concept into chunks: the natural urge to survive, the chemicals that create the good feeling that our survival needs are met, and the pathways that control the chemicals.

You can help others notice their expectations about meeting their needs. These expectations are the source of our safe and unsafe feelings. It's hard to put our expectations into words, but we have power over them when we do. Talk is a tool that expands our awareness of our nonverbal impulses. Talk helps our horse and rider understand each other. In daily life, only a small part of your experience gets put into words. So, when your horse gets triggered, your rider has trouble finding the reason. When you talk, your rider stops doing other things and focuses on the horse's perspective. Your verbal brain discovers the patterns being activated in your mammal brain. Once your verbal cortex gets hold of a thought, you have more power over it. The cortex can turn things around and look at them from different directions. You can look at something in a way that feels safe.

We all have old patterns we'd rather not talk about. Talk can activate the pain of the original experience. We avoid pain, so we are good at avoiding thoughts of past pain. The bigger the pain, the bigger the circuit we build to detour around it.

Such detours are easy to imagine for dramatic traumas like a near-fatal accident or early abuse, but small irritations build them too if they're often repeated in youth. For example, if you repeatedly felt put down when you were young, every detail of that experience can trigger your pain circuit. In adulthood, you find yourself avoiding such details and don't know why. Just the thought of approaching them feels extremely threatening. You presume the threat must be real because the feelings are so strong. Talk can help a person uncover the powerless child who stored the reactions, and reexamine the situation as a powerful adult. Talk helps you chart the roads so you can build the extensions you need.

A simple example is the pain caused by the adolescent urge to be "cool." No one likes to think this motivates them in adulthood, but big circuits build because the mammal brain creates life-or-death feelings about social importance. These big circuits get in your way when you need to do something that's "uncool" by the standards of your adolescence. Going to bed early, for example, triggers your adolescent pain circuits. You can end up harming yourself with a sleep deficit because your mammal brain is so motivated to avoid being "uncool." This loop is hard to escape when you can't admit that it's happening.

You can help a person discover his or her adolescent circuits and redirect them. While it's hard to talk about this vulnerability, it's easier to talk about it in monkeys. Adolescent monkeys didn't go to your high school, yet their challenges feel curiously familiar. At a certain age, elder monkeys withdraw protection and a young monkey must meet its own needs. It faces competition from stronger individuals. It has a sense of urgency about social rivalry because its genes are annihilated if it fails. It is not thinking about its genes; it is trying to feel good and avoid feeling bad. Anything that feels good is very motivating.

You have to get comfortable with your own adolescent template before you can help someone else. We are all sensitive about the suggestion that we are shaped by our adolescent reward structure. We blame our fear of being uncool on society, or we ignore it entirely. You can help others make peace with their adolescent template by presenting it in a safe way. You can help them understand the navigation system they wired in long ago, with all its superhighways and detours. You can help them find their power to build new pathways by stepping in new directions. It's hard to do this with mere words, so we are fortunate to have nonverbal tools as well.

MIRRORING

We all mirror others without conscious awareness. We choose what we mirror instead of mirroring everything. A fascinating study with monkeys explains how we do it. Scientists showed monkeys an image of a person's hand grasping a mug of juice, and the monkeys' mirror neurons activated. But when the monkeys saw an image of a hand in the same grasping position but no mug of juice, no mirror neuron activated. Obviously, it's about the juice. Our mirror neuron system evolved to notice the rewards and pain experienced by others because that information promotes survival. It has become fashionable to call this "empathy," but it's essential to know that your brain seeks information relevant to your own survival.

You can help others discover new rewards by experiencing rewards in front of them. When you take pleasure in vegetables, or cleaning your desk, or socializing without artificial stimulants, you help others activate that pleasure. If you tame anxiety with the three-step tool, you help other learn to focus on what they want, give their cortisol time to dissipate, and take their next step. "Actions speak louder than words" is an old saying with a sound neurological basis.

When appropriate, you can share your anxiety-taming practice with a person you want to help. You can share thoughts about what you want, include that person in your distracting activity, and bounce ideas about your next step. Your pleasure in that step will spark the other person's pleasure, building positive expectations about the next step.

Whether it's appropriate depends on your relationship with the person you want to help. Professional relationships have limits, and personal relationships have limits. But with a bit of strategic thinking, you can design effective mirroring opportunities for the person you want to help. Instead of modeling a behavior yourself, you might help a person locate situations where the desired behavior is on display. These efforts will be well-rewarded because mirroring penetrates the mammal brain in ways that verbal preaching does not.

Undesirable behaviors are always on display too, of course. If you are trying to lose weight, everyone else seems to be licking an ice cream cone. But if you stand in front of an ice cream shop, you are causing that undesirable modeling. You can help others notice when they are standing in front of an ice cream shop. You can show them how different the world looks a few feet away. When people say "everybody does it," they think it's a fact because of their mirroring choices.

When a person feels anxious, it's easy to say "everyone is anxious." You can help a person discover a new universe of behaviors to mirror.

The power of mirroring is interesting to see in horses. When a group of horses runs together, the leader is in the center rather than in the front. The other horses are mirroring it. You may think the leader is in the center because of high-minded motives, but the leader is in fact only promoting its own survival. The center position is the safest from predators, and ungulates invest their strength in a quest for a more central position. When a threat is perceived, a strong and confident individual chooses its steps and others mirror it. This is how a horse leads from the center. When you take calm, confident steps, you are leading from the center.

People mirror what you do rather than what you say, of course. Their mammal brain zooms in on how you get rewards and how you avoid pain. If you do one thing and say another, you teach people that insincerity is a way to get rewards or avoid pain.

If you tell someone to relax but you are not relaxed yourself, you will not help that person tame anxiety.

This happens a lot, of course. We try to calm others because it helps us meet our own needs. When we make others responsible for our anxiety, we teach them to abdicate responsibility for their feelings. This is probably not what you want. With careful planning, you can model a tame response. It's worth the effort, because mirroring can carve new paths in the back-roads of the mind.

CARROTS AND STICKS

It's hard to change emotions because they rest on pathways built from past experience. New pathways can be built from new experiences, but activating new experiences with old pathways is a challenge. Carrots and sticks can help. Carefully planned rewards and pain will trigger new chemicals, which build new expectations.

This strategy is controversial. The stick is no longer acceptable, and even the contingent use of carrots is widely seen as objectionable. I am not advocating actual sticks, of course, but social pain is very powerful. You don't want to inflict social pain on others, but they are already shaped by the social reward structure of the world around them. You are already rewarding some behaviors and not others. You can pay closer attention to the reward structure you are creating and fine-tune it to align with your anxiety-taming goals.

Often, we reward bad behavior without realizing it. We give more attention and respect to behaviors we don't want than behaviors we want. Despite good intentions, we teach people that bad behavior gets social rewards. With more awareness, you can direct your attention and respect toward behaviors you want to encourage.

This is often harder to do than we expect. I was reminded of that when I took my husband horseback riding. I had gone on trail rides with my father when I was a kid, and I learned that a trail horse expects to be fed when it returns to the barn. If you let it feed on the trail, it has no incentive to keep stepping. My husband had never been on a trail ride, though his father grew up on a farm, while mine was from Brooklyn. He let his horse munch on grass whenever it wanted. Our group leader told him not to do that, but my husband couldn't bring himself to discipline his horse. Soon, the horse refused to budge and our whole group was stuck. Finally, the group leader came and took over the reins. My husband learned to fear trail rides, but he did not learn to discipline a horse.

We are all tempted to reward bad behavior because it feels so good in the short run. When you offer acceptance or respect to an angry or anxious person, you feel like a good guy. When you withhold it, you risk being branded a bad guy. Thus, you are really focused on your own needs when you reward bad behavior, even as you invoke a higher purpose. It takes a strong focus on long-term goals to transcend this impulse.

You have probably heard that rewards are bad because they undermine intrinsic motivation. The studies that purport to prove this have a problem, however. They talk about "intrinsic" motivation without acknowledging that such motivation was produced by the child's past experience. A child who was rewarded for bad behavior in the past will revert to that when left to follow their "intrinsic" motivation. They need to experience a new reward structure in order to escape that loop. They need to enjoy new carrots for new behaviors and lose old carrots for old behaviors.

We often hear that "the squeaky wheel gets the grease." It makes sense to grease a squeaky wheel, but greasing a squeaky human has unintended consequences. If you are nicer to the angry person than you are to the pleasant person, you teach people that anger gets rewarded. If you are nicer to the anxious person, you teach people that anxiety gets rewarded. You can help others by scrupulously noticing your social rewards, and resisting the urge to reward bad behavior.

Foreign languages are best learned through immersion because you have to speak the language to get rewards when you live in another country. You get food and make friends when you speak the words, and your brain links the words to the good feeling of meeting your needs. Real rewards are more motivating than books and tests. This doesn't work if you meet your needs in your native language while immersed in a foreign land. Our brain learns from the behaviors that actually get rewarded.

Rewards are valuable because they can motivate small steps that add up to big steps. Animal trainers call this "shaping." They reward tiny steps as long as they are steps in the right direction, and soon, a complex behavior has been "shaped." For example, a pigeon will spin in a circle if you reward it every time it turns its head in one direction. The pigeon keeps repeating the head turn to get another reward until it has completely spun around. If you tried to teach a spin from the start, the pigeon would not understand what behavior is needed to get the reward. You have to break the desired behavior into steps that are within its experience.

You must be consistent in your use of rewards to avoid the problem known as *variable reinforcement*. A gambler at a slot machine is a well-known example of variable reinforcement. So is a child having a tantrum or a criminal planning another heist. When a behavior gets rewarded some of the time but not always, the mammal brain tries harder instead of giving up. Research on pigeons, rats, and monkeys makes this clear. Thus, if you reward bad behavior occasionally, the bad behavior gets entrenched. You must resist rewarding bad behavior all the time in order to change expectations.

Carrots and sticks have power. You can help a person with carrots and sticks by carefully planning your contingencies and sticking to them.

You may long to "help" a person by granting a reward whether or not the person executes the appropriate behavior. You may hate to withhold rewards from anyone. You may even pride yourself on finding new ways to justify rewards. This does not help the person you purport to help. It only helps you.

WHEN "HELP" DOESN'T HELP

The world is full of would-be "helpers" who reward bad behavior. Parents, teachers, managers, and public servants reward bad behavior more than they realize. They want to meet their own needs and feel like a good person. They want approval, even from those they purport to help. So they perpetuate a dysfunctional incentive structure and ignore the consequences.

If you truly want to help, look carefully at the behaviors you are rewarding. It's hard to violate your sense of magnanimity in the short run, but you can focus on the long-term benefits. Imagine all the future pain you are relieving by helping a person build healthy expectations about rewards.

Let's return to the uncomfortable topic of sticks. We do not use sticks in today's world, even for animals. But pain can contribute to a healthy reward structure in other ways. The pain of hunger motivates a horse to return to the barn. Feeding a horse when it strays from the path causes problems. A rider must make careful decisions about rewards and pain in order to reach a destination.

You can help others by withholding rewards until they have met explicit criteria. Maybe you'd rather protect them from the pain of disappointment, but that would not help them. By holding them accountable, you help them build a skill, find their power, and enjoy the pleasure of their own steps. When you reward bad behavior, you make it harder for them to find their power.

When other people reward bad behavior, you notice. It's easy to criticize the perverse incentive structures effected by managers, parents, teachers, leaders, and counselors around you. But when you reward bad behavior, you feel like you are just being a good person. You end up reinforcing the expectation that bad behavior is a good way to meet needs. You would help more by doing nothing.

The urge to rescue others is natural. It puts you in the one-up position without risking your acceptance and belonging. You stimulate serotonin without losing oxytocin, which is hard to do in other ways. No wonder it's so popular.

For most of human history, it was so hard to survive that you had limited energy to rescue others. Today, many people have a lot of energy left after meeting basic material needs. They have more energy to invest in the quest for social rewards. Thus, we have a lot of people looking for someone to rescue.

The urge to rescue is easier to understand in a historical context. In past centuries, sailors couldn't swim; even ships' captains couldn't swim. If you lived in those times, you might dream of rescuing people by putting life guards on every ship. You might imagine a huge global program with massive funding for life guards. You might not think of teaching sailors to swim because that skill was not widespread in your experience. And you wouldn't want the sailors to feel blamed or judged for not swimming. You just want to help.

If you really want to help, teach someone to swim instead of providing life guards.

REMEMBER:

1. Anxiety is hard to tame with words because it's hard to find the connection between the verbal brain and the chemical brain. You can help people discover their nonverbal impulses through the act of finding words to associate. You can help them access the verbal brain's power to look at an impulse from different directions.

2. You can help others activate the feeling of confidence in their steps, and repeat it until the pathway builds. With conversation, you can help them locate that feeling in their past experience and understand the need for repetition.

3. Positive expectations relieve anxiety. You can help others identify their expectations so they have power over them. You can help them recognize the adolescent experiences that built their expectations.

4. Mirror neurons activate when we see others get a reward or risk pain. You can help people discover new rewards by experiencing those rewards in front of them. If that's outside the bounds of your relationship, you can help them find useful models.

5. We are always making choices about what we mirror. You can help others notice their choices and redesign them.

6. Pay careful attention to the behaviors you are actually modeling, because the person you want to help is likely to be mirroring them. Your actions count more than your words.

7. The brain learns from whatever gets rewarded. We often reward bad behavior, despite our best intentions, because it helps us meet our own short-run needs. You can help others by carefully aligning your rewards with desired behaviors.

8. Rewarding small steps toward a desired behavior can shape a big new pattern.

9. Rewards must be consistent. If bad behavior is rewarded some of the time, it will persist. Variable reinforcement motivates a mammal to work harder to get a reward it has gotten in the past.

10. It feels good to rescue others and it feels bad to withhold rewards from others. You must understand your own feelings about helping others in order to truly help.

EPILOGUE

As I write this, I await the arrival of my first grandchild. Her parents want her to be happy, and so do I. But I have learned more about the brain since my kids were young. I will not rush to pick up a toy that my granddaughter drops. I know she will be happier in the long run if she picks it up herself.

The urge to protect children from distress is very strong. We want to give them what we want, and we want relief from distress. We fear terrible consequences if we fail to relieve their distress. And if the Joneses protect more, we hate to protect less. I am not advocating neglect, of course. I am advocating new insights into what makes a child happy in the long run.

The best thing children can have is confidence in their own skills. To build those skills, they need experience. The best gift we can give them is respect for their ability to manage their experience.

No one is born with the skill of feeling safe. Each brain must build self-soothing skills from its own experience. Having perfect experiences is not what creates a sense of safety. It happens when a child builds trust in its ability to meet its needs. Each time a child decides what it wants and takes steps to get it, the circuit builds. When a baby's ball rolls away, it figures out how to crawl because it wants the ball. A child needs to want something to release the chemicals that motivate action. With repeated action, confidence builds.

The best way to help a child tame anxiety is to tame your own. Mirror neurons are nature's teaching tool. Face disappointment with calm confidence and your child will do that too.

My grandchild cannot be born with confidence in her steps. She can only build confidence in her steps. She has to build the neural pathways that choose her steps and the pathways that trigger positive expectations about them. She'll need repeated experience to build those pathways. Fortunately, she can enjoy the experience. I can't wait to see her figure out what to do when her ball rolls away.

BIBLIOGRAPHY

Ardrey, Robert. *The Territorial Imperative*. New York: Dell, 1966.

Berger, Joel. *The Better to Eat You: Fear in the Animal World*. Chicago: University of Chicago Press, 2008.

Brown, Eva Marian. *My Parent's Keeper: Adult Children of the Emotionally Disturbed*. Oakland, CA: New Harbinger, 1989.

Cheney, Dorothy, and Robert Seyfarth. *How Monkeys See the World*. Chicago: University of Chicago Press, 1990.

Conniff, Richard. *The Ape in the Corner Office: Understanding the Workplace Beast in All of Us*. New York: Crown, 2005.

Darwin, Charles. *The Expression of Emotions in Man and Animals*. London: John Murray, 1882.

DeWaal, Frans. *Chimpanzee Politics*. Baltimore: Johns Hopkins University Press, 1982.

Gilbert, Paul. *Depression: The Evolution of Powerlessness*. New York: Guilford Press, 1992.

Keizer, Garret. *Help: The Original Human Dilemma*. New York: Harper Collins, 2004.

McGuire, Michael, and Lynn Fairbanks. *Ethological Psychiatry: Psychopathology in the Context of Evolutionary Biology*. New York: Grune and Stratton, 1977.

McGuire, Michael, and Alfonso Troisi. *Darwinian Psychiatry*. New York: Oxford University Press, 1998.

Palmer, Jack, and Linda Palmer. *Evolutionary Psychology*. Boston: Allyn & Bacon, 2002.

Roe, Anne, and George Gaylord Simpson, eds. *Behavior and Evolution*. New Haven, CT: Yale University Press, 1958.

Roth, Kimberlee, and Freda Friedman. *Surviving a Borderline Parent*. Oakland, CA: New Harbinger Publications, 2003.

Stevens, Anthony, and John Price. *Evolutionary Psychology*. London: Routledge, 1996.

Trivers, Robert. *Social Evolution*. San Francisco: Benjamin-Cummings, 1985.

Wilson, Edward O. *Sociobiology: The New Synthesis*. Cambridge, MA: Belknap Press of Harvard University, 1975.

INDEX

addiction, 78–79, 106, 109–10
adolescence. *See* puberty
adrenaline, 13–14
alarmism. *See* declinism
alcohol, 79, 86, 91
animal training, 19, 53, 137–38

boredom, 109

Cannon, Walter B., 13
childhood, 2, 9, 16–17, 20, 30–31, 36,
    43–44, 48, 50–51, 64, 69–71, 82,
    84, 90, 93–96, 110, 115, 121, 127
children. *See* childhood
clutter. *See* decluttering
comedy, 37, 89, 92
common enemy, 31, 68, 72, 111, 116
competition, 31, 33, 45–46, 68, 95,
    113, 115, 134
conflict, 26, 32, 97, 98, 112, 124
cortex, 11, 21, 39, 52–53, 61, 80–82,
    100, 110, 112, 115, 133
cortisol, 3–4, 8–9, 12, 14–20, 22, 31,
    35–36, 38–39, 43, 46–47, 51, 61,
    76, 79–80, 84, 87, 99, 107, 109–10,
    125, 127
Csikszentmihalyi, M., 80

dating. *See* reproduction
death. *See* mortality
declinism, 70, 83, 101, 115–16
decluttering, 1–4
disappointment, 1, 21–23, 35, 46,
    64–65, 67–68, 99
divorce, 27, 83
dopamine, 28–30, 35, 39, 46, 58–59,
    62, 64–65, 67, 71, 75–76, 80–81,
    83, 87, 89–90, 106, 109, 115,
    121–23

Ellis, Albert, 108
endorphin, 28, 34, 92, 126
energy, 22, 29, 33, 47, 50, 53, 65–68,
    77, 79, 82–83, 94, 100, 123,
existential angst. *See* mortality
expectations, 28–31, 33, 35, 38,
    45–46, 53, 58, 64, 68–69, 75, 90,
    95, 97, 99, 115, 124, 133
eyes, 13–14, 18, 20, 54

fear, 3, 13–14, 69–70, 80, 98, 120–21
fight-or-flight, 13
food, 7, 8, 15, 22, 29–33, 63, 70, 72,
    79, 81, 91, 96, 105–6, 111–12,
    119–29

foreign language, 37, 89, 113, 132, 137

free time, 3, 5, 21, 96–97

habituation, 75–78, 91, 102, 126–27

hedonic treadmill, 76

help, 45, 85, 107–8, 131–38

horse and rider, 7, 19, 39, 43, 45, 67, 70, 108, 133, 136–37

intrinsic: motivation, 137; muscles, 92

laughter, 34, 92

limbic system, 7–8, 21, 52, 82

mirror neurons, 16, 89–90, 102, 111, 115, 131–36, 140–41

money, 39, 52, 62, 65

moral superiority, 33, 84

mortality, 3–4, 14, 82–83, 116

muscle tension, 92, 109

music, 36, 62, 80–81, 88–89

myelin, 43–44, 48, 50_51, 54, 64, 71, 78

natural consequences, 70–71

neural pathways, 9–10, 16–20, 29–30, 54, 61, 64, 78, 107, 114–15

neurons. *See* neural pathways

oxytocin, 28, 30–32, 35, 46, 58–59, 62, 67, 71, 77–78, 83, 85, 87, 107–8, 115, 124–25

pain, 16, 18–19, 31–32, 34, 38, 69–70, 89, 109–11, 133, 136

pets, 7, 36, 88

puberty, 44, 51, 78–79, 111, 114, 134

reciprocity, 98–99

reproduction, 7, 10, 13–14, 27, 32–33, 51, 82–83, 100, 111, 114

reptiles, 17–18, 50, 112

rewards, 8, 19, 22, 29–30, 35, 48, 53, 55, 58, 64, 69, 72, 75, 78, 87, 89–90, 97, 99, 122–23, 127, 131, 135–38

rubber ducky method, 93–94

Sacks, Oliver, 52

serotonin, 28, 32–35, 46–47, 58, 62, 67, 71, 77–78, 83, 85, 87, 107–8, 115, 125–26

sleep, 71, 100, 134

smoking, 23, 53, 55, 97

social: comparison, 3, 33, 66, 84–85, 90, 110–14, 126; dominance, 32–33, 83, 110, 113–14, 126; pain, 20–21, 23; status, 32, 84–86, 107, 111–15, 125–26; support, 2, 31–32, 67–68, 93–95, 107, 110, 124

sympathetic nervous system, 15

synapse, 54–55

tension. *See* muscle tension

trust, 28, 30–32, 39, 68–69, 80, 91, 94, 116, 124–25

variable reinforcement, 138

zoo, 11, 17, 53, 55, 119–20

KEEP IN TOUCH

Loretta Graziano Breuning is founder of the Inner Mammal Institute and author of *The Science of Positivity: Stop Negative Thought Patterns by Changing Your Brain Chemistry* and *Habits of a Happy Brain: Retrain Your Brain to Boost Your Serotonin, Dopamine, Oxytocin and Endorphin Levels.* She is professor emerita at California State University, East Bay. The Inner Mammal Institute offers resources for rewiring your mammalian neurochemistry. Breuning writes the blog  *Your Neurochemical Self: Getting Real with a 200-Million-Year-Old Brain* on PsychologyToday.com. She has been interviewed on NPR, *The Matt Townsend Show*, and the *Ask Altucher* podcast, and her work has been featured in *Psychologies*, *Real Simple*, the Dodo, Independent Voter Network, and the School of Life in London. Breuning currently lives in Oakland, California. She wants to hear about your success in taming anxiety. You can write to her at Loretta@InnerMammalInstitute.org.